THE VANQUISHED

A DOUBLE D WESTERN

In 1857 "manifest destiny" was a way of life for men of initiative and courage, not just a slogan of vote-hungry politicians. To the ninety Americans in Senator Crabb's expeditionary force, the march into Mexico—to assist the Mexican rebels in overthrowing a dictatorship—seemed like a once-in-a-lifetime opportunity to make their dreams come true. The lure was a promise of liberal settlement rights in the land to the south.

So confident were the leaders and men of the well-equipped, well-organized expedition that they could almost taste the fruits of victory . . . But at the end of their march across the burning Arizona desert was a rendezvous with death at the bullet-scarred church of Caborca.

 LOOK FOR THE DOUBLE D BRAND

THE
VANQUISHED

Brian Garfield

DOUBLEDAY & COMPANY, INC.

GARDEN CITY, NEW YORK

1964

AUTHOR'S NOTE

Sixty miles south of the Arizona line, on the Rio de la Concepcion in northwest Mexico, a forgotten church stands crumbling on the outskirts of the old town of Caborca. The remains of its walls are pocked with the tracks of bullets. Flood waters have eaten away much of the structure, even to the dome, and those parts that have been rebuilt in the last decade seem awkward and cheap beside the older, more artful work of the eighteenth-century padres who originally built the church. The religious life of the town has moved to a new central plaza a mile away, where an ungainly new church stands in pale imitation of the old structure.

The church was built by Franciscan priests on the ruins of a mission established by Padre Eusebio Francisco Kino, S.J., probably in the 1690s. Roundabout grow the palms of Caborca, tall trees; for the age of a town in that isolated desert country is measured by the height of its palms. Some of them today reach upward more than a hundred feet. Their fruit is used year-round; their leaves make thatch, their trunks timbers.

On the church is a bronze plaque, erected April 6, 1926, to commemorate an event that took place seventy years earlier.

> *Humbly we pay grateful homage to*
> *the army of Mexico and the men of*
> *Caborca, who on April 6, 1857, made*
> *this temple stand as a bulwark for*
> *the defenders of the fatherland by*
> *inflicting defeat on the North Amer-*
> *ican filibusters.*

vii

When Mexico wrenched its independence from Spain, the northwestern state of Sonora was crippled. Its wealthy dons, loyal to the Spanish crown, closed the rich mines of Sonora and destroyed all their equipment before they fled. Sonora, once a flourishing frontier province, suffered abrupt privation. Apache marauders from the north swept through the district in brutal raids, butchering the inhabitants; in self-defense, the Mexicans hired ruthless scalp hunters and offered two hundred dollars' bounty for the scalp of every male warrior brought in by the contract hunters. These hunters—men like James "Don Santiago" Kirker and John Joel Glanton—soon discovered that it was easy enough to pawn off the scalp of a peaceful Mexican citizen as Apache, and thus collect their bounty without endangering themselves. At the same time, parties of North Americans on their way to the California gold fields trooped through northern Sonora, treating the natives with contemptuous cruelty.

It is no wonder, then, that by the late 1850s North Americans had earned a bad name in Sonora.

The state itself, effectively cut off geographically from the rest of Mexico by the menacing ramparts of the Sierra Madres, was an isolated community, ripe for the ambitions of a dictator. Such a man was Jesús Gandara, who bought and held by force of arms the governorship of Sonora. By bribery and threats, Gandara secured an alliance with the local commander of federal troops, General Yañez, and with the chief of the Yaqui Indians, El Indio Tanori. Even today in Mexico the mountain Yaquis are considered a dangerous threat. They are the only Indian tribe who have never signed a treaty with either the United States or Mexico; technically they remain at war with the whites. As late as 1929 a skirmish took place at Nogales between Mexican Rurales and a Yaqui band.

With such fierce allies, Gandara held Sonora firmly.

A revolution was brewing against him in the mid-1850s, led by a resolute colonel of militia, Ignacio Pesquiera. To aid his cause, Pesquiera enlisted the help of Henry Alexander Crabb, a California State Senator and Pesquiera's relative by marriage.

Thus it was that one of the most daring of the nineteenth-century filibustering expeditions was organized. The strange tale of Crabb's filibuster begins in Sonora, California, and ends in Sonora, Mexico. It is the story of ninety men who marched across the burning desert Camino del Diablo (Devil's Road) of Arizona toward a rendezvous with death at the bullet-scarred church of Caborca.

*   *   *

As a historical note, the story here told is a true story. All the important events are related with as much accuracy as possible in the light of the varying versions of the affair that have come down to us.

Theoretically a novelist has a vaguely defined area of license into which he can incorporate his fictions. An attempt has been made to minimize that area in this novel: all characters are real except for a man named Cassio and three or four women; few liberties have been taken with facts, and none at all with significant events or dates. Of course dialogue, description of many details, personalities of most characters, and other minor matters are products of the author's imagination, just as the meaning of the story must be a product of the reader's.

Documented historical sources for this story, while not widely known in the popular sense, are plentiful and easily available. It seems needless to list them here, but of course the author retains a complete bibliography.

It remains only to be said that my indebtedness is very great to Jesus Y. Ainsa, to the library of the University of Arizona, to Dr. Robert H. Forbes, and, as always, to the Arizona Pioneers Historical Society, which houses Dr. Forbes' massive collection of materials dealing with the Crabb Filibuster Expedition. I am indebted as well to my friend Henri L. Castricum of Tucson.

B. W. G.
Paris, 1964

THE VANQUISHED

CHAPTER 1

Charley Evans stood on the half-rotted boardwalk in a driving rain and watched the Abbott-Downing stagecoach lean away from the depot and pitch toward the head of the street, its seventy-five dollar mules straining in the mud. Rain battered his hatless head and glued the shirt to his back.

If the present was dismal gray and the future a probable black, and the past a kind of dusty sad yellow, then Charley would choose the pale past, bleak as it might have been. The sun rose and set; life until today had been a matter of mornings beginning darkly before dawn, and evenings chiefly remembered for exhaustion. If most youths of sixteen had the mirage of a vast shining future luring them on, such visions had faded for Charley Evans. For the most part the pleasantest part of the day had been the few minutes he could steal away from swamping in the Triple Ace Saloon to be with his careworn memories. There was a girl over the mountains in Stockton; her name was Maria and he thought a good deal about her. But that had been last summer, and by now she was probably fat.

Charley had worn a polish on these memories while he pushed his mop and avoided the insults and malicious slaps of Bill, the bartender. His eyes had grown gray and wise.

In the east, solemn gray became lackluster pink. This told him he was late for work, and he turned and took his tattered carpetbag along the walk toward the Triple Ace, forgetting for the moment that he did not intend to go to work today. He had the old carpetbag with him because he intended this to be his last day in the Triple Ace, or for that matter in this gray patternless town of Sonora. Recently, looking around him, he had decided that he had seen enough of the wonders of the California hills. Today or tomorrow he would go away on a trek, eastward. All he had to do was find someone headed that way. Today's future grew brighter in hue than yesterday's; he had a vision of great cities, wealth, opulent women.

A loose board gave way under his heel. It almost upset him. He cursed mildly and went on, turning his eyes along the street with the wise glance of a father. There was a strange thing in the sky—in the east the dawn was wide and pink, but in the west where the sky was still dark, the moon seen through haze was a sharp-rimmed disc of pale white. Overhead pendulant thunderheads concentrated above the center of the valley. Raindrops made him blink. He came along the muddy walk to Jim Woods's saloon and intended to go by the place, but the friendly Woods came out as far as the awning's shelter and stopped him with an amiable inquiry: "All packed, I see. Going somewhere, Charley?"

"Back East."

"You're doing the Triple Ace out of a chore boy, then."

"They'll find another one."

"I reckon." Woods squinted toward the sky. "Funny-looking moon, all by itself," he observed, and tilted himself so that his shoulder rested against the weatherbeaten post that supported the awning. Rain pelted it overhead and Charley tarried under the shelter. Woods' eyes were overhung by thick gray brows; he had an idle air. "Tired of the job, Charley?"

"You might say."

Woods smiled absently. His skin seemed as raddled as old leather; his muscles were hard. Charley wondered how old he was. Woods asked, "Got money for the trip?"

"I'll work my passage."

"That's a hard row," Woods said conversationally. "Ever done much wagoning?"

"I've done most everything, one time or another."

"Cross country ain't the same," Woods warned him. "It's hard luck, boy. A lot of bones bleaching on that trail."

"All right," Charley said, "then I'll learn something new."

"I guess you will," Woods said. Charley had him marked as a friendly harmless man. "Good luck to you, then, Charley."

"Thanks," he said, and went on up the street with his carpetbag, a solid youth, five and a half feet high and thick-chested. The shirt clung to his back; he owned no coat. The carpetbag weighed little. He bounced it by the handle in his fist, and swung up along the glistening brown ribbon of the street, past crowded buildings and corrals, and paused again under a long sagging balcony at the next intersection. The Triple Ace was a drab building across the brown, limpid trough of the street, its faded sign flapping on rusty chains in the rain. In the doorway stood the thickset bear-shape of Bill Randolph, the bartender. Bill was a sadistic soul. Without noticing Charley, he turned back inside and the door slammed. Charley stood where he was. A businessman came waddling along the walk, loose coat flapping, beaver hat dripping. The eastern sky was turning sickly yellow. Charley pinched his lips, thereby giving his face a waspish expression, and stepped down into the ankle-deep mud. It was red-brown in color, and clung to his boots, restraining him. He tramped struggling across to the gray face of the saloon, and stopped outside; and then impulse turned his steps away, and he went quickly back the way he had come, going into Jim Woods's saloon.

The room was heavy, musty, full of odors of stale whisky and dead tobacco smoke. The wood-framed clock behind the bar ticked loudly. Lamps flickered dimly along the walls. He found it no brighter than it had been outside in the bleak dawn. Rain dappled the high roof with sound. He stood just inside the door, the threadbare carpetbag dangling from his grip, and ran fingers back through his long ash-colored hair, splashing water down the back of his neck so it wouldn't drip in his eyes.

Woods was nowhere in sight; there were no customers. The saloon was a big silent cavern until the front door squeaked open. Charley stepped aside and saw a long-fingered man in the doorway removing an oilskin slicker. The man doffed his hat, batted water from it, and went up to lay his slicker across the bar. He wore a black coat, and underneath that a yellow pinstriped shirt. There was a big revolver in his waistband. The

3

gleam of his eye-surfaces matched the hue of the shirt, and now those yellow eyes flicked coldly past Charley.

Woods came in through the back door and put on a friendly look. The yellow-eyed man said, "Hello, Jim."

"Why," Woods said, "hello there, Norval. I didn't expect to see you this soon."

Thereupon the two men settled into a conversation. Uncomfortable, Charley advanced to the bar. Woods looked around and said, "Morning again, Charley."

Charley said, "You haven't got a sandwich left over from last night, have you?"

"I reckon," Woods said. "Stay put a minute, Norval. Charley, this is Norval Douglas. Norval, Charley Evans." He went back.

Norval Douglas put out a hand toward Charley. His handshake was quick and strong. He tipped his hat back and a shock of hair dropped across his forehead, black and straight. At the temples it was shot with gray. It was a country of bearded men but Douglas was shaved smooth along the high cheeks and the shelf of the long jaw. Two deep lines ran from beside his nostrils to the corners of the mouth; otherwise his face appeared young.

Abruptly he said, "How old are you, boy?"

"Going on sixteen."

"I guess some men are born old," Douglas observed. "You show more years than that."

Woods came back in with a tray of sandwiches. The bread had turned hard, edges curled up, and the salt pork was bitter, but Charley ate with hunger. Woods said to Douglas, "Charley just quit his job."

"That so?" said Douglas. "Made any plans?"

"Thought maybe I'd hook up with a freight outfit going East."

The yellow eyes bobbed around from Charley to the rainy street, and back to Charley. Douglas's long fingers scraped his jaw. With thumb and forefinger he flicked dryness from the corners of his mouth. Woods set a mug of beer before him and Douglas picked it up, and said, "Any particular reason for going East?"

"I've got tired of it here."

4

"This town's as good as any," Douglas suggested.

"All right," Charley said. Woods was drifting back along the bar, doing some kind of work there. "What of it?" Charley said.

He observed the constant traveling of Douglas's wary glance. The yellow eyes came around and for a long interval his glance clashed with Charley's, and Charley began to feel a pale red anger: he met those yellow orbs precisely midway and answered them with a challenge of his own. Douglas produced a briar pipe, packed it from a yellowed leather tobacco pouch, and used a flint-and-steel mechanism to light it, all the while maintaining the grip of his eyes on Charley's.

"What the hell?" Charley said.

"You'll do all right," was the answer. Douglas's expression, like a natural law, seemed to leave nothing open to question. He nodded and considered the glowing bowl of his pipe. Charley noticed the big six-shot horse pistol that sat at hand in Douglas's waistband. "I'll do all right for what?"

"How long have you been looking out for yourself?"

"Long enough, I guess." He saw the gentle upturn of Douglas's lips and added, "A few years. Odd jobs, mostly."

"No folks, Charley?"

"I ran away."

"And stayed away," Douglas said. "That takes a little courage. What are your plans?"

"I just told you."

"I don't mean just that," Douglas said. The pipe had gone out; he ignited it again. A thin column of yellow-gray smoke lifted from the bowl and even as far up as the high ceiling Charley could see the smoke fan out and crawl along under the boards, seeking escape. A man and a woman, arm in arm, went by outside, the man holding a parasol over the woman's head. Norval Douglas said, "What do you expect to make out of yourself?"

Charley thought about it. "I don't know."

"You intend to drift along?"

"Isn't that what you're doing?"

5

"Now," Douglas murmured with a quizzical little smile, "what makes you guess that?"

"You look like you've been around some," Charley told him.

"For a fact," the yellow-eyed man replied, "I have."

"What for?"

Douglas seemed to know that the tables had turned on him, but he showed no reluctance to answer Charley's question. "There's some satisfaction in traveling over the world when you know you don't have to become part of any place. You see things, you learn things—but you're not touched by them unless you want to be. You see?"

"Maybe," Charley said, not altogether sure. "But when you get all through, what have you got?"

"The most precious thing of all," Douglas said quietly. "You've got yourself—you know what you are."

"All right," Charley said. "What are you?"

"A man. All by myself."

"That's fine," Charley said drily. "Must be kind of lonely."

"It is, until you learn that you don't need anything from anybody." Douglas glanced back at his horse and sucked quietly on the pipe for a moment, and said, "How would you like to go to Mexico?"

"What for?"

"To stake a claim. Build a home and make plenty of money."

"Sure," Charley said. There was a slight caustic edge on his voice.

Douglas showed a brief smile. On his face, a touch of restlessness, a touch of isolation. Tough, he appeared, but at the same time mild. There was evidence of quiet humor in his eyes. "Think about it," he said. "There will be plenty of profit in it for you—if you're willing to do a little fighting."

"Against who?"

"Indians. Mexicans, maybe. Probably not, though. There will be a good many of us." He turned to leave. "I'll be here if you decide to come along with us." Saying nothing more, Douglas put his yellow eyes once more on Charley, and went out.

6

Charley watched him go, slicker flapping in the rain, until the lean figure disappeared into the gray gloom.

Woods came forward again and put his elbows on the bar, and said, "Fine fellow, that one."

"You know him well?" Charley asked.

"Hard to say," Woods said cautiously. "Sometimes I doubt I know anybody very well. People are hard to make out, sometimes. That's something you'll learn when you get a bit older, I reckon."

"I already learned it," Charley said, and left the saloon.

Over the mountains he could see slanted shadowy streaks of falling rain. On the veranda of the Overland depot a fat drummer sat with his sample case in his lap and a bulging suitcase by his feet. An ore wagon drawn by eight teams of oxen wended a slow track down the street; the bullwhacker's livid calls echoed down the street. Two intersections up the street, near the Triple Ace, Charley turned off into a narrow alley. The air was still damp and cool but the sun now shot its rays down between buildings and the clouds were beginning to break up, receding southward, and he came to a little white frame house with pink-lavender curtains showing in the windows. Beyond this point were the scattered tents of the back of the town, littered in a patternless disorder. Charley turned up the stone-bordered walk of the little white house, passed between two precious strips of lawn, and knocked.

When the woman opened the door, Charley said, "Hello, Gail."

"Well, hi," she said. Her eyes were a pale agate in color, a little sharp, perhaps brittle. Her body was full-molded against the calico dress and she smiled a bittersweet smile, stepping aside to let him enter. He went inside, standing uncertainly with his carpetbag until she said to him, "So you're leaving us?"

"I guess so."

"Good. Good for you. If I had the guts and the money I'd go with you. I'm sick of this town—I'm weary of fools."

She went on; she always dropped into these periods of feeling sorry for herself. He stopped listening after a while. On the

7

round table was a mahogany music box with a cameo scene of a snow-blanketed farm implanted in its upraised lid. He saw a dark feather duster standing in the corner and, beside it, a woven carpet beater. It was a homey kind of room. He could relax in it, and that was a rare luxury for him.

From his chair he could see into the kitchen—the coffee mill with its drawer half open, the round-bellied stove. On the table beside him there was a mustache cup. Her voice came back into his awareness: "Sometimes I think I hate everybody."

"I know how that feels," Charley agreed.

"That's a crying shame. You're too young to be that way."

"So are you. So's everybody, I guess. How old are you?"

"I don't know," she said. "Maybe twenty-five. When do you figure to leave town?"

"Soon as I can."

"Well," she said abstractedly, "remember me, will you, Charley?"

"I guess I will. Maybe I'll write you a letter."

"I didn't know you could write. I can't write."

"I'll get somebody to write it for me."

"You do that, Charley."

"I will," he said, knowing he never would. The whole hour was lame and very sad. He stood up and took his carpetbag to the door. "Well, don't let anybody push you around, Gail. Listen—thanks for everything, hey?"

"Women like to play mothers," she answered. "Maybe it's the only chance I'll ever have. You don't have to thank me."

"Thanks anyway," he insisted.

"Charley."

"What?"

"Do you need anything? Money or food or anything?"

It brought him up. "Why'd you say that?"

She turned half away and put her hands on the lid of the music box. "I don't know, maybe I like you too," she said.

"Why? What for?"

"You're a good-looking fellow."

"Yeah. Well, thanks."

8

"Maybe I like to see something clean once in a while. You're still clean, Charley. Stay that way, will you?"

"Sure," he said.

"Good luck."

He nodded. "So long." He made a vague signal and went out. A cool wind had sprung up, it brushed his face in the alley. He heard the music box tinkling its tune and when he looked back he saw Gail in the open door with a sad smile on her face. Her shoulders stirred faintly; she pulled the sleeves of her dress up. The air had a bite in it. He went out of the alley's mouth, back into the street, and stood undecidedly watching the town. A scatter of horses stood around at the rails, hipshot and half asleep, now and then blinking or kicking or swishing away flies with their tails. The light mudwagon mail coach from the Sacramento run rocked around a last bend of the coach road into the head of the street, came forward bucking and scratching up mud, and pitched to a stop at the depot. The drummer on the porch picked up his sample case and carpetbag and walked to the coach, and waited. Front-lifted buildings with a beaten look lined the thoroughfare, and an enormous man walked across the street into the Triple Ace. The sky was fairy blue. Clouds were a mass southward; it was still raining down there, but several miles away. Puddles in the street flickered. A group of horsemen, Mexican *vaqueros*, breasted the foot of the street and drummed forward, arriving in a swirl before the drygoods store, dismounting there. Charley went stiffly down the street, again tightening apprehensively when he went by the Triple Ace, and felt his mind going around in aimless circles.

The word SALOON was painted across the face of Jim Woods's place in a crescent shape. When he stopped before the open-top doorway of the room, a stale weight of tobacco smoke and men's bored droning voices rolled out past him. With several unconnected thoughts idling through his mind, he tarried briefly where he was, then turned with a half-brisk snap of his young-wide shoulders and pushed into the place.

He found Norval Douglas sitting behind a table, with a solitaire game laid out half-finished in front of him, and a mug half

9

full of beer idle by his forearm. Douglas's yellow eyes lifted and acknowledged Charley's presence, and Douglas said, "You want the job?"

"I don't know."

CHAPTER 2

Henry Crabb's eyes were deep and dark and brooding, set back in hollow sockets. His beard was dark brown and he had a habit of stroking it with his left hand when he was in thought. He sat in the deep-red overstuffing of the chair and looked across the plush parlor through the bay window, out across Market Street at the hazed-over waters of San Francisco Bay. Wind rustled the branches of a maple tree outside the window; it was mild for a winter's day. Across the room, seated stiffly in a cane-bottom chair, was the Spaniard, Hilario Gabilondo. Gabilondo was awaiting Crabb's reply, and held his neck rigid while he tried unsuccessfully to contain his impatience. Farther back in the poor light, Filomena sat quietly with her hands folded, and, looking once at his wife there on the divan, Crabb softened his expression just a little. She smiled wistfully. Beside her, her brother Sus watched from under heavy brows. Sus sat with one lanky leg thrown irreverently over the arm of his chair; when he noticed Crabb's glance on him, his teeth flashed out of his dark face in a friendly, easy-going smile.

Crabb returned his glance to the window and considered the mists over the waterfront. He could barely make out the island. His eyes settled on that faint blue-gray outline; his hand tugged at his beard. He was thinking not so much of Pesquiera's offer, to which Gabilondo, having delivered it, now expected a reply; Crabb was thinking more of little faraway things, like the croaking of bullfrogs in the dark bayous and the smell of honeysuckle on a porch in Nashville. But Nashville and the Baton Rouge bayous were half a continent and many years away, and just now he should not be drifting toward those things, and so he dragged his mind away from these little pleasantries and hauled in the anchor of his attention, allowing it to drag back to the mustached, sun-brown face of Hilario Gabilondo.

"Señor," Crabb began, and in the corner of his eye caught his wife's slight quizzical smile—Crabb spoke very little Spanish, and she liked to chide him for it—"Señor, let me understand you properly, in simpler terms than I find in this flowery document." The document was in Spanish, and he was not confident of his reading of it. Gabilondo smiled courteously and leaned forward a little in the cane-bottom chair. He seemed perched on the edge of it in a subservient yet mocking manner. Crabb dipped his head and looked inquiringly at the Spaniard from under his heavy, lowered eyebrows.

"Has Señor Ainsa read the agreement?"

"I'll read it now," Sus said, lazily uncoiling and getting out of the chair. He came forward with his indolent long-legged stride, all his joints loose, and took the paper scroll from Crabb. Then Sus stood by the back of Crabb's chair, his hand on it near Crabb's head, while he read. Meanwhile, Gabilondo was talking in his smoothly accented and half musical voice:

"The agreement provides that in return for the arms and supplies that you propose to supply us with, you will receive the right to establish a colony of six hundred families in Sonora. Of course this will not be until we have secured office. It further provides that you are free to choose your own site for colonization, and that if your site is privately owned, our government will pay the purchase price on behalf of your colony. You are offered a year's free subsistence for your colonizers in return for protecting our citizens against the Apaches from the north. We offer no scalp bounty—we have found too many weaknesses in that venture."

"I can understand that," Crabb said politely. At his shoulder, Sus finished his reading of the Mexican document and handed it to Crabb. With nothing more than a brief nod, Sus went back across the length of the room to his chair, where he resumed his original position, leg draped over the arm. Crabb tugged his

11

beard. Irritatingly, images and memories clouded his thoughts. He had to push away a recollection of young people singing by dim lamplight on a manor's wide veranda.

"Through me," Gabilondo went on, "Ignacio Pesquiera asks your help. Another gain you will make will be the recovery of the properties in the Arizpe district that were lost by the family of these two kind people at the time of our revolution." Gabilondo bent his head toward Sus and Filomena, who represented the dwindling power of the Ainsa family. He added, "That is the sum of our agreement. Do you accept it?"

"It merely restates my original proposal to Pesquiera," Crabb said in a muffled tone. "It's entirely acceptable. Of course I'll agree to it."

"Very well, then." Gabilondo displayed all the stiffness and exact-courteous airs of a hostile diplomat; Crabb disliked him heartily. But he was accustomed to dealing with political men, and showed none of his distaste. He said, "You'll find the arms and ammunition in a warehouse at the foot of Front. Here's a bill of lading—you can advise me if the shipment is satisfactory."

He stood, withdrawing a yellow document from his waistcoat pocket, and crossed the room with choppy strides to hand it to Gabilondo. The Spaniard glanced up at him and read the bill of lading carefully. Presently his dark head moved up and down and he folded the paper, pocketing it. "*Bien*," he murmured. "Our fight against Gandara goes well. This will make the victory more quick and more certain. You have our thanks, señor. How soon may we expect your colonists?"

Crabb glanced through the window and returned unhurriedly to his red chair, and sat before he spoke. "My men are recruiting people for an exploratory party now. We should be able to embark within the week. I intend to take a party of about a hundred men on this first trip. That will be large enough to protect your flanks from the Apaches, and at the same time secure a site for our colony. Afterward we'll send for more colonists, with families. I don't believe women and children should be subjected to the rigors of the first expedition."

"Of course," Gabilondo murmured. "I understand perfectly, señor."

"Once your revolution is ended, and we have established accommodations for our people, that will be time enough for the families to join us."

"Yes." Gabilondo stood up, a stocky brown soldier, holding his beaver hat. He moved to the door, turned to bow low to Crabb's wife, gave both Crabb and Sus his short, firm handshake, and left with a frigid white smile on his dark face.

When the door closed, Sus sank back into his chair and considered his fingernails with lazy-lidded eyes. "I do not trust him. He's a *ladron* if I ever saw one."

"You make use of whatever you have to work with," Crabb told him. "Sus, you'd best make ready to start our journey."

"My equipment is already packed," Sus said without looking up. Indolent as he seemed, he had a way of accomplishing things. He said, "I believe I shall pay a call on a young lady. If you will excuse me?" He smiled roguishly toward his sister, touched Crabb's arm in a friendly way and strolled out.

Crabb stood with his hands behind him, regarding his wife gently. "Filomena, your father will be pleased that we're acting to return his lands to him."

"He is weary of all that," she said. "I don't believe he cares much any more."

"I'll wager he'll be pleased, just the same," Crabb said stoutly. "Come here to me, my little bird."

Her slight, willow figure came erect and advanced gracefully. She smiled for him and he thought that she was a very pretty woman. "Little bird," he murmured, and kissed her lips with gallant tenderness, holding her chin with his forefinger.

Afterward he put a hand to his beard and let his gaze wander absently under a lowered frown, and said, "I shall have to see Cosby immediately. I'll be back presently, my dear."

Her eyes followed him as he took down his greatcoat and hat from the foyer pegs and went out into the brisk damp push of the wind.

He signaled a hack at the corner of Sacramento Street, and

13

rode over the steep-tilting cobblestone avenues past many rows of misty wooden houses perched on the slopes like balanced rocks, until the hansom soon drew up before a brown wooden house and Crabb stepped down, paid the cabbie, and walked carefully around a puddle while the hack went clopping down the street.

General Cosby's door was at the head of six broad weather-beaten steps. Crabb swung the knocker four times and stood tugging his beard until the door opened and the yellow-skinned houseboy took his coat and hat and led him into the parlor. The general's desk commanded one wall, beside the deep-scalloped window. The view was a bleak row of wooden houses marching down the street's grade like a mammoth stair.

General Cosby, loose-paunched and shirtsleeved, sat behind the desk sweating at the armpits. His short-cropped black beard made his face seem even rounder than it was; his eyes were small bright buttons set close together behind a pince-nez with octagonal lenses. His greeting took the form of a grunt. "Hello, Henry."

"Enlist your army," Crabb said with force. "We're about to move, my friend."

"How's that?"

"Gabilondo just delivered Pesquiera's agreement to me. The matter is settled."

Cosby leaned back and pursed his lips into a little rosebud, as though whistling. "Think of that," he said.

"Do," Crabb said drily.

"Well, that's good," Cosby grunted. "Now we can be getting down to work. Sit down, Henry, and we'll discuss the plans."

"Aagh," Crabb said in friendly disgust. "You haven't a bone of joy in you, old friend."

"There's time for that kind of thing. Afterward."

"Can you comprehend celebration? The occasion calls for a drink, I'd say."

"Very well. Chan?"

The houseboy appeared in the doorway, his face round and flat and wholly expressionless to the eye. "Two brandies," Cosby said gutturally, and the yellow face disappeared from the door. "Now," Cosby said.

"Relax a moment, can't you?"

"Why?"

It took Crabb aback. "Must you always push, my friend?"

"Until the objective is accomplished, an officer should not rest," Cosby said. "All that comes to an idle man is whiskers."

Crabb shook his head with a bemused smile. "We've gained something important today—can't you see that?"

"Henry, you strike me at this moment as an eager young dog—you have all the bounding enthusiasm of one. But there's much yet to be done. We can't sit back and count our rewards yet—we haven't won them."

"You always prick at a man's pleasures," Crabb complained. The houseboy entered on padding feet, stolidly carrying a silver tray on which were balanced two goblets of brandy, deep and richly brown. Crabb accepted one and held it in the air. "To our success in Sonora."

Cosby took a quick swallow and set his glass aside on the polished surface of the desk. He adjusted the pince-nez on the bridge of his nose and used the flat of his hand to rub his belly with large, circular motions. He was, Crabb thought, disreputable in appearance and manners; but he had been a good soldier and his strategic wisdom was valuable. Cosby said, "I've just received the latest communications from the correspondents in Nicaragua. William Walker's filibusters have taken over the government there and President Pierce gave formal recognition to Walker's regime. But the Costa Ricans are up in arms and the most reliable estimates are that Walker's position is precarious, at best."

"He failed before," Crabb said, "in Baja California. He's an unstable man. We can't count on him."

"Well," Cosby observed, "it was his idea, anyway—not ours. I'll be satisfied with a good deal less than Walker dreams of."

"It was largely a pipe dream anyway. To take over all of Mexico while Walker moves north—to have our two victorious armies meet at Mexico City and proclaim the whole of Mexico and

15

Central America a new republic—the idea was absurd, old friend, but I enjoyed the pleasures of speculating upon it for a while. No, I'm afraid we must confine ourselves to more modest gains. We haven't the resources to recruit a force large enough to defeat Mexico, and the Mexican War is too recent in American memories. I doubt we could interest Washington in another war."

"I've reached the same conclusion," Cosby said. His grunting manner of talk was almost animal in nature, Crabb thought; but he put away his dislike of the man because more was at stake than personal feelings. "Walker," he said, "will have to look out for himself."

"Then that's settled." Cosby removed the pince-nez and blew on the lenses and set the device once more on his nose, and lifted his button eyes to Crabb. Crabb crossed his legs and went loose in the chair, gently swirling the brandy in his goblet and watching the brown liquid lick toward the edges of the glass. He said, "As we planned, I gave Gabilondo the excuse that we didn't wish to subject women and children to the rigors of the overland journey. That should adequately explain why we'll be traveling as a party of well-armed men only."

"All right," Cosby said. He lodged his thick elbows on the desk and used a pencil to draw aimless sketches on a notepad while he talked: "You'll sail by the end of the week, then. I anticipate it will take you at least two months' time to travel from El Monte overland past Jeager's Ferry to the Concepcion. Meanwhile I'll be gathering my force—say a thousand men—and I'll sail around into the Gulf. We'll land at Port Lobos and make our way upriver. I'll expect to meet your column at El Altar or Caborca. By that time Pesquiera should have done a fair job of destroying Gandara's power, and with any luck at all we should find Sonora in a state of abject confusion. I don't expect much difficulty when it comes to unseating Pesquiera, if we have to, but I hope he'll see our side of the matter and recognize that he'll be better off with us than against us. It's unfortunate we had to arm his men, but I suppose it's the only way to cut down Gandara's army. I must admit, though, that there are a few minor weaknesses in the plan."

"To wit?"

"What will your father-in-law think of our venture, once he finds out what we're really doing?"

"He'll still be getting back the properties that the Mexican government stole from him. I doubt he'll complain. He seems to have lost interest in Mexican affairs."

"Getting old, is he?"

"Yes."

"Then," Cosby said, "what about your wife?"

"Allow me to handle my own domestic affairs," Crabb said, a bit drily. "My wife owes no particular allegiance to the Mexican government."

"But she's still related to Pesquiera."

"I intend no harm to Pesquiera, unless he demands it. He won't—he's a reasonable man. We'll offer him a good position in our government, once we've set it up."

"All right," Cosby said, standing up and thrusting his hand forward across the desk top. "I'll have a thousand men well armed and ready to meet you at El Altar. But you've got to secure the foothold before we arrive."

"Done," Crabb said, and met Cosby's eyes while he shook hands.

CHAPTER 3

The meal hung heavy and soporific in Charley's belly. He had a glimpse of his long-boned face in the backbar mirror and considered the dour hang of his young-old features while Norval Douglas spoke to him and Jim Woods stood by Douglas, listening.

Douglas was saying, "For the moment, we wait."

"What for?"

"Senator Crabb. He should arrive shortly. He's been in San Francisco, organizing his backers." Douglas's attention turned to Woods, who was raking hard-knuckled fingers through the length of his beard. "Made up your mind yet, Jim?"

Woods moved his grizzled head, looking around the half-empty room, sweeping the bar and tables and hardwood floor. "A long time," he murmured. "This was the first saloon in Sonora town —the first one in Tuolumne County, for that matter. It took four of us three weeks to throw up the original building." His attention dropped to the bar and he pounded softly with his fist. "At first this was just a couple of planks we threw across some kegs. A long time, Norval. Damn near eight years ago—we got here with the first of the rush, late in 'Forty-nine. They used to hold miners' court in here—did you know that? Vigilantes hanged a man from that rafter, in 'Fifty-one."

"That was the boom," Douglas said. "I remember it."

"Sure. You had to pay ten dollars for a pair of fried eggs. It's my feeling the gold will peter out soon. A good many of the camps have already died, and I expect this town will turn ghost too, one day. Sure, Norval—the fun's gone out of these hills. I've made and lost half a dozen fortunes in this place. All gone now."

"Mexico has rich enough lodes," Douglas said mildly. "Rich enough for everybody. That will be your wages down there—a mining claim in return for your gun. Are you game?"

Jim Woods's shoulders lifted and dropped. "I've let grass grow between my toes long enough, I guess. Maybe I could build me a little cantina down there. Sure, I'll come along."

"Good enough," Douglas said. "You want a drink, Charley?"

Charley lifted his head. "What?"

"Want a drink?"

"Why," Charley said, "I guess I will. Thanks." It was good to be treated without the kind of humoring deference that most men paid to youths. He saw the closeness of a smile behind Douglas's even glance; he accepted a drink from the bartender and sipped from it. Across the room a frock-coated professor was pounding the spinet, and on the sawdust square a number of miners danced in grim fury with the girls. The girls were powder-pink of cheek and had brittle, calculated laughter. When Charley looked at Douglas again, the smile had gone from those yellow eyes and Douglas said, "How about it, Charley?"

"I ain't decided yet."

"We may be moving out soon."

"I'll let you know."

Douglas nodded. "What about your folks, boy?"

"Never mind them."

"Where are they?"

Charley shrugged. He turned around and leaned back on his elbow and watched the dancers—clumsy stamping men and girls whose smiles turned to grimaces when their faces were averted. Charley said, "The old man had a place over on the south fork of the American River, last I heard."

"You don't see much of your father, is that it?"

"He's not my father."

"No?"

"Stepfather. He's a Creole my old lady picked up in New Orleans."

"That where you come from, boy?"

Charley looked up at him. "That's right. What are all the questions for?"

Douglas tilted his hat forward over his brow. His smile removed certain rough edges from his face. He said in a soft drawl, "I just like to know what kind of a man stands in back of me, Charley. No offense."

"I haven't said I'd be in back of you, yet."

"All right." Douglas opened his flat-shelfing jaw wide to yawn, arching his back and blinking with comfortable satisfaction. "The land and the mines are free for the taking. We'll colonize the place, that's all. But I've seen Apaches and I know what they can do. Jim, you make damn sure you can handle a gun."

Woods looked straight at him. "Yeah," he said huskily.

Charley said to Douglas, "Tell me something."

"What's that?"

"Why are you in this thing?"

19

Douglas considered it. Above the high bones of his cheeks, his powerful eyes were two symmetrical slits. Charley saw the fighting streak along his mouth. Back in the saloon there was a quick clashing of voices, overridden by the twang of the spinet. "Well," Douglas said presently, "you've got to function. I mean, a man's a functioning being. If you don't function, you're not a man any more. Nothing means anything until you step out and act. You've got to act, and you've got to believe that your action means something—you've got to believe there's a point to it."

"What's the point of it?"

"Yourself," Douglas said. "Myself."

"I don't follow you," Charley told him.

"Look at it this way. Down in Mexico, all that land, all those minerals—that land is there to be used. It's there for you and me to make something of it."

"Why me and you?"

"Charley," Douglas said, and paused, looking down at his hands as though carefully composing his words. "Maybe you're not old enough to understand this yet."

"Try me."

"Don't you ever feel impatient about something, when you want to be in motion, you want to get something accomplished?"

"I guess so. But I'm still way behind you."

"Maybe you have to be," Douglas murmured. "You're still young, you're still threshing around, looking for solid ground. You'll find it, sometime. You've got the bones of a man. But remember one thing—the greatest failure of all is failure for the want of trying."

"What?"

"Keep hold on the truth. You're the master of your world, Charley, as long as you live by and for your own life. There's a lot of time in the day. Cover it at a steady pace, boy, and use it like a tool. Don't lose it—don't squeeze yourself flat. When you see a chance, take it."

"Like Mexico?"

"That's it," Douglas breathed. "A chance like this one. If it's not too late. Maybe I've wasted too much of my damned life already. I've drifted around from camp to camp and army to army. I've fought Indians and panned gold, dug furrows and hauled freight. A lot of time goes by and you learn how to do this and that, and how to handle men. But all the time, Charley, the answer's right there—in yourself—if you look for it. Traipsing over the hills is a waste of time. Figure yourself out right now, boy. Don't wait twenty years."

Charley couldn't tell if it was the whisky talking, or a wash of bitter memories, or in fact the zealous conviction that it seemed to be. Douglas was hard to figure out. Most of the time he seemed supremely sure of himself, almost to the point of arrogance. Charley didn't know. He had never troubled to ask himself what he was doing or why he was doing it, or what would come of it; until now, he had never concerned himself with the possibility that his life might have a meaning.

"I'll think on it," he told Douglas, and went from the bar.

*　　*　　*

To Charley, Crabb looked about thirty-five. He was not a particularly tall man. He talked with a clinging drawl; Charley had learned the man came from Nashville. Just now, Crabb stood on a platform of knotty planks surrounded by banners of the Whig party and the American party and a painted wooden sign with his own long name spelled out, HENRY ALEXANDER CRABB. Jim Woods read these words aloud to Charley. Up on the platform Crabb stroked his bushy goatee, threw his shoulders back and launched into his speech.

Charley had heard several politicians speak, most of them office-seekers passing through town campaigning. Crabb's speech started off a good deal like all the others. He used a full stock of the old familiar vague words that were meant to give people a comfortable feeling of well-being and warmth. He talked about destiny, justice, protection, patriotism, sacrifice—words that meant everything and anything, words that meant perhaps one thing to the politician speaking them and altogether a different thing to the people listening to him.

21

And the odd thing, Charley thought, was that both the politician and the crowd were wrong, dead wrong.

The words issued sanctimoniously from the lips of the politician, who had probably never explored their real meanings, and the words fell on the crowd like water to cleanse their souls, to apologize, to make repentance for them, to reassure them that *they* were not to be held responsible for whatever evils they had caused by refusing to trouble themselves to reason. And then the words would be flushed away, as Charley had swept away mud and debris from the floor of the Triple Ace—day after day he would clean the floor, and day after day men like politicians would leave new deposits of filth.

The speech troubled Charley, and while Crabb spoke with massive gestures and glistening teeth and sharp-shining eyes, Charley began to consider more carefully the proposition of Douglas, the yellow-eyed adventurer. He did not wish to be led into trouble by a velvet-tongued politician. He knew that in Texas, the Mexicans had allowed *Norteamericanos* to colonize —and a war had resulted. Charley had listened to a great many men in his short term of life, and from what he had learned he knew enough to distrust the kind of piety that Crabb just now was preaching. It was far easier to trust a man like Norval Douglas, who was tough but direct.

Then, with a barely perceptible transition that Charley almost failed to catch, Crabb was talking to the crowd in wholly different terms. Charley's attention now fixed itself more closely on the man and he listened with more care.

Crabb stood with feet braced a little way apart, a blocky figure in a brown broadcloth suit. His heavy arms rode up and down, injecting hot impatience into his talk; and his deepset dark eyes were bright.

"My friend Ignacio Pesquiera, gentlemen, is now seeking to overthrow the forces of Governor Gandara. The fate of the province of Sonora depends on the outcome of this struggle. I can assure all of you who choose to follow me that Señor Pesquiera's gratitude will be richly bestowed on all those who give him assistance in gaining the governor's palace."

"Listen to him," Jim Woods said drily into Charley's ear. "Richly bestowed, he says. From what I hear, that's a hell of an understatement."

"Mexico," Crabb went on in a deep, round tone, "is in a state of political upheaval today, and the man who holds a governorship is a powerful man indeed. There need be no question in your minds that Señor Pesquiera can well afford to repay those to whom he is indebted, just as soon as he takes control of the province."

"If he takes control," Woods murmured dourly, and someone beside him said, "Shut up."

Crabb was continuing. "I have with me, if you want to examine them, agreements from Pesquiera himself, whereby every man in my party will be granted both mining concessions and extensive land tracts in northern Sonora, near the boundary of the Gadsden Purchase. I'm sure you are all aware that the gold deposits of northern Mexico are second to none in the world—not even those of our beloved California."

"Beloved, is it?" Charley muttered. He had to move aside to see past the head of a tall man. The sun struck the earth and crowd and the smell of unwashed bodies was strong when the breeze lulled. Crabb paused to sip from a glass. His eyes went along the crowd and Charley tried to make out the meaning of the man's set expression—was it contempt or only earnestness? Crabb said:

"A few years ago, Sonora was one of the richest provinces of all Mexico. Today vast *ranchos* stand deserted, mines lie idle but rich, unclaimed cattle roam the plains by thousands, and all this great land stands ready for us to take it. All we have to do, my friends, is be prepared to stand fast against the Apaches. It is the Apaches who have laid Sonora waste, and it is the Apaches from whom we must reclaim it. This is the task Pesquiera wishes of us—and, gentlemen, it is a task for which he is willing to pay."

Crabb's pause was obviously meaningful. The day was warm for January; the sun was made of brass. Crabb swept the crowd with his chin-firm glance and said in a lower tone, "Think about it, gentlemen. My men are among you, ready to take down your

23

names. We will be happy to have all of you—there is more than enough for all, where we go."

Back in the crowd, some fool began to applaud, and the hand-clapping took hold and pounded in undulating waves of sound against Charley's ears until Crabb stepped down from the platform amid that steady roar. The gold camps were playing out; Crabb had found a willing audience for his promises of wealth and booty. The applause dimmed quickly until there was only one man smacking his palms together, and that too stopped quickly, as if the unseen man had noticed his own foolishness. Somewhere nearby in the crowd a coarse voice said, "They got pretty women in Mexico. I always was partial to that brown meat." The man laughed shortly. "Gold lyin' all over the ground, boys. Oil your guns, hey?"

Charley turned away with his head bowed in thought. He was suspicious of it all; something about it did not ring true; he did not know exactly what it was.

The crowd slowly shattered into small groups, each one a nub of excited conversation. Men drifted away in all directions. The recent storm had left the streets hard-packed and rammed firm, and there was little dust. Jim Woods, grizzled and hard-muscled, was going downstreet with a small group, all of them talking impetuously, gesticulating and laughing heartily. Crabb had disappeared, along with the frock-coated men who had shared the platform with him. A large figure filled the doorway of the Triple Ace—Bill Randolph, the bartender. Charley's throat tightened and he turned, going down the walk toward Jim Woods's place.

At a corner table, Norval Douglas sat behind a large ballot box and a number of sheets of paper and quill pens. Douglas was busy recruiting; a queue formed quickly enough and grew until it extended almost to the door. Douglas was studying the face of each volunteer and every now and then he would shake his head and say a few curt words, and the applicant would curse him or go slack-jawed or simply shrug and turn away. Charley went to the bar, where Woods waited with a half-amused expression on his seamed-leather face and a beer mug in his fist, and Charley regarded the anxious line of volunteers with troubled uncertainty. He said to Woods, "What does Crabb get out of this? I don't figure him for the kind to settle for a gold mine or a ranch he'd have to work."

"He's the leader," Woods said. "He'll be the top man of us —in Mexico he'll be able to speak for all of us. Some men need that kind of power. Besides, his wife's an Ainsa."

"What of it?"

"You know the Ainsa family?"

"Rich crowd up in San Francisco, aren't they?"

"They are now," Woods said. "They used to be a lot richer, when they was in Sonora."

"What happened?"

"Politics," Woods said. He had a time-weathered face and a way of chewing periodically on an imaginary cud. "When the new bunch grabbed the governorship down there, and the revolution ended, the Ainsa family got kicked out of Mexico. The government confiscated all their property. Crabb's made a deal with Pesquiera to get all that stuff back for his wife's family. Happens Pesquiera's related to them."

"How'd you find this out?"

Woods shrugged. "I don't expect it's any big secret. Besides, when you run a saloon as long as I have, you develop a pretty good ear for news."

Charley looked across the room at Douglas. Woods said, "Want a beer?"

"No." Tobacco smoke was strong in his nostrils. "One thing rubs me. What if Pesquiera doesn't win? What if Gandara keeps control?"

"That's a fact," Woods murmured. "Think about this, too. What if Pesquiera wins the fight and then decides he don't need us any more?"

"Sure enough," Charley murmured. He looked at the diminishing line of men enlisting at Norval Douglas's table. Douglas's eyes came up idly and met Charley's, as if by accident; Douglas's eyebrows lifted questioningly, but Charley made no response of any kind. He turned and walked thoughtfully out the door and up the street. A long-slanting beam of sunlight cut through the western clouds to splash a faint redness on the town; in the quickening dusk, Charley looked up into an indigo sky and filled his chest with air.

CHAPTER 4

Coronel Señor Don José Maria Giron was troubled. He did not have the heart of a true *revolucionario*. He was a soldier, not a dealer in intrigues. And what troubled him even more was that today he and his detachment must guard from the enemy the person of Ignacio Pesquiera himself. The whole of the matter played on Giron's nerves.

Pesquiera was not very old, but his long beard already had a stringy and gray look to it. It was his fierce eyes that held you, that made you know that he was a man born to lead. Today he sat upon a round-smooth rock, his legs drawn up and long arms wrapped around his knees, and looked down through the trees at the wooded course of the river, the Rio de la Concepcion. The way he held his head and the way his eyes flashed indicated to Giron that the man might as well have been sitting upon the throne in the Governor's Palace at Ures. Pesquiera would be there soon, too. Nothing was able to stop him. Giron watched him and felt an immense respect for Pesquiera's leadership, for his strength and courage, for his wisdom. To Giron, a simple soldier, the man was great.

Scattered around through the trees, alert and armed, were the men of Giron's detachment, ready to lay down their lives to protect the person of Pesquiera from any sneak attack by the Yaquis or the *federalistas* or Gandara's private guard, or whoever was in the field under Gandara's orders. There were so many enemies it was hard to keep them straight—Governor Gandara had a fiendish skill when it came to welding together outlandish alliances. It was Giron's business today to protect Pesquiera against any or all of them.

He got up restlessly to pace the sloping forest floor. Below, in patches through the timber, he could see the river flash. The hot January sun beat down on all of Mexico, and particularly on Colonel Giron, who was a heavy man very much prone to sweat. His eyes were high and narrow, his cheeks round and his jowls soft and his mustache thick with a soldierly droop. His belly hung comfortably over the wide leather belt, and the skin of his face was very smooth and very brown. His fingers were stubby and thick, and played with the caplock of his rifle. Back in the woods squatted the patient *Indios*, the breechclouted savages whose job it would be to load the coming cargo of rifles and ammunition onto the pack animals and take care of those animals. The Indians were loyal to Pesquiera because they were paid to be loyal. It made Giron shiver even under the warmth of the sun; every loyalty was so tenuous. He had never been able to develop the calm attitude toward revolutions that his country-men adopted. Abrupt and frequent shifts of loyalty were not easy for Colonel Giron. He believed today in the republic, as he had always believed; for that reason he fought with Pesquiera against Gandara, only because Gandara had made of himself a dictator, and Pesquiera was a wise man who promised freedom to the people of Sonora. Giron stopped in a clear spot of sunlight and felt sweat drip from his armpits, staining the brown shirt he wore. Crossed bandoliers of ammunition weighted his heavy shoulders; the rifle was sticky where his sweaty hand held it.

"Gabilondo is late," Pesquiera said in liquid Spanish, and Giron saw the mark of impatience in the way Pesquiera's lips were pressed together. "We cannot wait forever in this place," Pesquiera went on. "It is too exposed. Gabilondo is an arrogant fool—does he believe he is free to keep me waiting all week?"

"I am sure he is making all haste, *mi general*," Giron assured him.

"Bah. I have never yet known him to make haste when his path had to take him through villages where there were women and *tequila. Mujeres y tequila*—except for these things, Gabilondo is a good soldier. But sometimes I could strangle him."

Giron said nothing; he only put his troubled glance once

more down the slope toward the trail that wound along the riverbank. The trees rustled gently in the wind.

Giron removed his big sombrero and wiped sweat from his face with his hand. Soon again it beaded on his lip and gathered in his eyebrows; there was no preventing the sweat. He cursed mildly and tilted his rifle muzzle-up against the trunk of a tree and hooked his thumbs in his belt. His belly hung over like a loose sack of meal. *I am heavy*, he thought. *Too much cerveza —but the beer is so good and a man has little enough pleasure.* Back in the woods the Indians shifted around—they were playing some kind of a game, throwing knives at tree trunks. They laughed and Giron swung—"*Sargento.* Keep the fools quiet. Do they want to bring Gandara's whole army down upon us?"

"*Sí, coronel.*" The sergeant gathered his legs under him and went yawning through the trees toward the group of Indians.

In the following silence a faint distant sound came to Giron's ears—the creak and sway of wagons. His head tipped up and he saw Pesquiera rising, standing on the rock bareheaded and gray, a tall man of Mexico. "It is about time," Pesquiera said testily, and came down off the throne of rock. "Come—we will go down to meet them."

"With care, *mi general*," Giron warned. By the time he had picked up his rifle and slung his sombrero across the back of his thick shoulders upon its throat string, Pesquiera was already going down the hill. Giron had to trot to keep up. He felt the loose fat of his belly bouncing. "General, suppose it is not Gabilondo? Suppose it is the *federalistas*? One should be careful."

"One does not win revolutions by hiding among the trees in fright," Pesquiera said contemptuously. Giron lifted his arm in a busy signal to his men, and felt somewhat reassured when he saw their white-clothed shapes flitting among the trees, coming down on either side with their weapons ready. He found himself puffing when they reached the bottom of the slope. Pesquiera stopped so abruptly that Giron almost ran into his high, broad back. "We will wait here," Pesquiera said, and put his shoulder against a tree and his hand on the butt of his revolver. Giron's worried glance traveled from the trail westward to Pesquiera's indomitable face and back again.

The noise of rumbling wooden wheels grew louder and presently the first of the pitching wagons appeared below, coming up the river. With considerable relief Giron recognized the stocky dark shape of Hilario Gabilondo astride the first horse. Pesquiera stepped out into the trail and held up his hand, and when Gabilondo rode up Pesquiera made one dry remark: "I see that you broke both legs getting here, my friend," and Gabilondo's only answer was a lazy grin and a wave of his arm toward the wagons that followed him. "The guns are here, Don Ignacio."

"Very well," Pesquiera grunted. "Have them unloaded and packed onto the animals. We will travel through the hills henceforth—Gandara's guerrillas still guard the main roads."

Gabilondo issued quick commands to his wagoners and stepped down from the saddle. He came forward leading his horse by the reins, and said with his stiff and precise voice, "The agreement was accepted by Señor Crabb." Giron noted a certain contempt in his tones. "He will come down with about one hundred followers, to pick sites and prepare accommodations for his colonists."

"Very well," Pesquiera said again. He turned into the shelter of the trees and stopped in the shadows, turning to look at Gabilondo. "What did you think of this man Crabb?"

"I do not like him—I do not trust him."

Pesquiera nodded. "He will be dealt with when the time comes. In the meantime, we must hurry these weapons to my men. With the aid of this new material, we should have the guerrillas driven far back in the Sierra Madre by the week's end."

"So soon?" Gabilondo said. "You have made rapid progress, then."

"We have." Pesquiera turned about and went up the hill.

Gabilondo came up, leading his horse, and put his distinctly unfriendly glance against Giron. "And how goes it with you, *coronel?*"

"Very well, thank you," Giron said stiffly. Gabilondo always drew him up and made him go taut in the belly. "Very well indeed, general." And he too put his back to Gabilondo and began laboriously to climb the hill.

*   *   *

William Walker had tried to colonize Mexico with a filibustering army; he had failed. De Boulbon too had tried in Sonora, and de Boulbon had died for it. Charley knew all this, and it did not help make his plans any more clear. After supper he encountered Norval Douglas on the street, and Douglas after fixing him with a cool yellow stare said, "How are you, Charley?"

"Tell me something. Why are you so anxious to get me to join up?"

"Not anxious," Douglas said. "Just interested. You're a good fellow, Charley. You stand on your own feet and you cast a shadow. If you want to know the truth, I see a lot of myself in you, when I was your age. I'd like to see you face up to something where you get a chance to find out about yourself. How about it?"

"I'm thinking on it," Charley told him, and went on. The smooth, pale surface of the street had a silver sheen in the moonlight. A dark, crowded bunch of saddle ponies waited riderless and slot-eyed patient along the rims of the street. A *vaquero*, mounted on a tall dark horse, left the stable and rode his animal into the street, his high-peaked hat silhouetted; the *vaquero* let go a long shout, wheeled his horse and galloped away drumming up the street. Standing in a window's pale beam, Charley looked back at the face of Jim Woods's saloon. He wished he had a way of knowing what to do. In the gloom of the saloon's shadow he saw a shape standing lean and vigilant: Norval Douglas.

At that moment Gail came along the street. She stopped by Charley and saw him looking at Douglas, and said, "Hello, Charley. Who's that?"

"Friend of mine," he said abstractedly. Down the street, Douglas pushed away from the wall and went into the saloon.

"Is that one of Crabb's men?"

30

"What?" He turned about. "Oh," he said, "yeah, he is."

"Don't do it, Charley. They're a bunch of toughs."

"Are they?"

"Do you have to ask me?"

"All right," he said. "What if they are?"

The fragrance of her hair reached his nostrils. He couldn't make out the meaning of her expression. She said, "You're better than that, Charley."

He uttered a crisp short laugh. "Sure," he said, "sure I am, I've got fifty cents in my pocket."

"Do you want money? I'll give you money, Charley."

He started, and for the first time put his whole attention on her. Her face was a sweet, solemn mask, willful and grave. He said, "What the hell for?"

She seemed remotely disappointed by his answer; she used both palms to smooth her long hair back. Her lips were set in a gentle way and the soft lamplight falling on her face made her flesh seem pale and smooth. She was not pretty; yet she had an arresting set of features. Her mouth was long, her nose uptilted, her cheeks a little hollow. But her eyes made her face appealing. Long, level eyes that glimmered. She was supple and round and she excited him, but out of a habit long ingrown he maintained his bleak old-eyed expression and merely said again, "What for? I'm just a shaver, remember? Wet and green."

"You look big enough to me."

"Sure," he said, and frowned when he looked away. He was not a stranger. He remembered the brown flesh of Maria, the contempt in her look. He had been down the trail and seen the cribs of Stockton and Sacramento. The body of a woman was a wonder and a mystery but not unfamiliar to him. He had only half a dollar in his pocket, and he knew Gail knew it. That was what puzzled him about the misty near-smile in her eyes, brightening the interest already there. "I ain't that big," he said, and saw her shake her head. The whores had laughed at him sometimes; they had seldom shown him any smile other than a calculated upturning at the lip corners and a brittle, weary look. *Maria*, he thought, and cursed inwardly. "What for?"

Whatever the answer was, it was only in her eyes, and he did not recognize it. He shook himself. "Aren't you supposed to be tending bar?"

"I let one of the dealers take over. I wanted some air."

"You've got it," he said.

Her laughter was soft and throaty. "Don't fool, Charley."

"What's that supposed to mean?"

"Don't pretend to be so hard. You're not that way."

"No?"

She laughed again. "No," she said, in mocking echo of him. She directed one long-lashed look at him and said, "Where will you sleep tonight?"

"I don't know. I sold my shack two days ago. Maybe in the stable loft."

"That's cold at night," she said. "Use my house. Here's the key."

The iron key dropped into his palm. When he looked up she was going away, back up the walk to the Triple Ace.

Lights sparkled out of windows. A small bunch of men came up the street, laughing and talking with hearty familiarity. They went past and left in their wake the residue of their laughter, soft and insolent and sour like a taste on his tongue. He stood alone in the shadows and beyond the roof of a low, flat building across the street he could see the branches of a tall tree swaying in the wind. The cool air bit through his clothing. It was a lonely hour. He puzzled, frowning, and presently settled his flat-slab shoulders, turning along the street. When he passed the stable's big open doorway, an earthy scent, damp and dark, issued from it. He tarried there. A dark tomcat shot out of the adjacent corral and spurted across the street. Wind made a thin hollow sound along the street; he was a solitary warmth in the night until a lantern came bobbing forward through the stable and the Negro hostler stood holding it shoulder-high. Its wavering flare glistened off the dark surface of his skin and eyes; his teeth flashed. "Howdy, Charley."

"Howdy."

"Fixin' to spend the night up here? I don't mind."

"I guess not," Charley said. "Obliged anyway." He went away, with the upraised lantern casting his shadow before him so that he trampled it into the dust when he walked. He turned into the narrow alley and walked slowly through it to Gail's little white house, and went in, using the key she had given him. Inside, he lighted a lamp and set it on the central table and turned its wick down low, and settled on a stuffed chair, from which he regarded the motionless, closed door through half-lidded eyes. Uncertainties troubled him, and too restless to lie still, he went to the door and flung it open and stood with the night wind brushing his cheeks. The image of a face wavered before him, temples shot with gray—the hard-eyed face of Norval Douglas. He thought of Douglas and thought of the man's toughness and self-assurance, and wondered whether he should follow Douglas. Cool air freshened his skin and now he thought back to his brother Ed, and the thinking was not new. Ed was in his grave now, but that was of no matter. Charley remembered in detail the day Ed had left home. Ed had come out of the barn with the horse he had bought from Pizner's neighboring farm, and Charley had come out of the house in time to see Ed's belongings loaded on the saddle and Ed leading the horse up to the shack, a tall youth with long ash-colored hair like Charley's own; Ed had called out to the house, and then Charley's father had come out, his Creole stepfather, and behind him Charley's mother had appeared timidly in the doorway, saying nothing, only putting her bleak hollow eyes like dead eyes on Ed and holding Charley's shoulders with her veined knobby-fingered hands. Charley had smelled the odor of whisky strong on his stepfather and he had listened wincingly to his stepfather's tyrannical voice, strange and always unfamiliar with its French-Indian accents: "Put up that horse and unpack those things. There is much work to be done and the Lord did not make you to idle away time adventuring."

Ed's answer had been gentle but firm. "I'm leaving, old man."

"The Lord will punish your soul. Have you a soul, Edwin? No matter—you'll be punished." His stepfather had drawn up

33

his thin shoulders and laid his glance like a whip with flat righteousness on Ed. "Unsaddle that horse now, boy!"

"No, old man."

His stepfather had clamped his jaws then and wheeled inside; and only then had his mother moved, lifting her hands reluctantly from Charley's shoulders and going down to stand beside Ed, touching his arm hesitantly and saying, "Go quickly—he's gone after the switch."

"Let him." There had been a grimness in Ed's eyes and Charley had stood back against the wall beside the door, watching with mute amazement. His mother had stepped away from Ed with fear on her face, and his stepfather had come out with the birchrod. Charley knew the sting of it. Now his stepfather had come down with the switch and Ed had stood his ground. His stepfather's demeanor was that of a man half raging and half drunk and when he had lifted the rod, Ed had jumped forward and pinned his arm, and Ed, with his face pressed close to his stepfather's, had spoken hissing: "You listen to me, old man. I've seen your pious preaching and your drunk crying and the way you like to push us all. I've seen it and taken it. I'm moving on—I don't expect you'll ever see me again, only if I ever hear you've hurt Ma or Charley, then I'll be back and I'll bust a hoe over your whisky-logged head. Now drop that Goddamned rod and step away from me, you old bastard."

It was the only time Charley had ever seen fear in the old man's eyes. The hand had opened, dropping the birchrod, and Ed had pushed the old man back, coming forward then and kneeling by Charley. He had put his hands on Charley's shoulders and said, "One day you'll be big enough to do the same thing, kid. I'll see you somewhere, when that time comes. But meantime you watch out for Ma and be a good kid, eh?" Ed had solemnly shaken his hand and wheeled abruptly to his horse, brushing the old man with his shoulder, and gathered the reins in quick synchronization with his rise to the saddle. The horse had turned and Ed had ridden away, followed by Charley's wistful eyes and his mother's rising tears and his stepfather's hoarse recriminations: "The Lord will avenge me! Let no man's son turn against the father—damnation upon the son—you shall lie in Hell!" And the old man's accent had made Charley want to laugh and want to hit him, to smash that red-lined face and crush it soft. The old man's arms had ridden up and down in exasperation and rage.

When Ed was out of sight down the fence-bordered road, the old man had turned and Charley had seen the angry round redness of his eyes. "Let no one speak his name in this house again. He is no son of mine."

"Neither am I," Charley had whispered, and the old man not hearing him had gone inside after his jug of corn.

The cold night wind slapped his eyes, making him blink. He stepped back into Gail's parlor and pushed the door shut and went back to the stuffed chair. In a moment he was up again, turning the lamp wick higher and carrying the lamp around with him while he searched the place and presently found, in a high kitchen cupboard, a clay bottle of forty-rod whisky. He took it down and poured a mugful and took the mug and the lamp back into the parlor, and sat up with his drink nursing it while he tried to push dismal memories away so that he could think about the good hours—riding the old bay plow horse up the riverbank toward town under a warm summer sky with dragonflies and bees making strange writings in the air and underfoot the passing of a broad field of brown-eyed yellow daisies. A hunting trip when he was ten, his brother showing him how to pour the powder down the muzzle and grease the patch and patch the ball and ram the ball home, halfcock the big knurled hammer and cap the nipple, set the front sight in the seat of the rear notch and draw his bead, and squeeze off the shot, afterward stepping aside to peer past the gently puffed cloud of black powdersmoke. Skinning an antelope out. Lying on his back under a silent temple of green treetops interlaced across the cloud-tufted sky, an ant crawling over the back of his motionless hand. Tramping through a fall of new clean snow to feed the stock in the barn. Skipping stones across the white-rippled surface of the river, deep water clear as sun-green glass. The smell of grass and wildflowers and pine needles, strong and heady the scent of the land.

The front door opened and Charley lifted his head sleepily in time to see the woman Gail slip inside and close the door softly. The pink-lavender curtains stirred. She turned to face him, throwing off her wrap, and said, "I thought you'd be sleeping."

"No."

She saw the mug in his hand and smiled. "You don't miss much, do you?"

He raised the mug to his lips and felt the amber liquid scald its way into his belly. When he put the mug down he grinned, showing his teeth. "I didn't figure you'd mind."

"Why should I? Help yourself." She sounded jaded. Through the crack-open window he heard the wind making a tune in the streets. She dropped her gray knit wrap on a table, put her level glance on him and let her hand hang idly touching the bundled wrap. Her lips parted, seeming to cling moistly to each other.

He gripped the whisky mug again, tightly in his fist, and suddenly he had the strange feeling that he was experiencing the exact moment when the fluidity of his youth was beginning to crystallize into its final form. The wind, no more than a gentle and almost imperceptible breeze, seemed quite distinct in his ears. His hand relinquished the mug and slid back toward him along the surface of the table. He noticed the yellow unsteady flickering of the lamp in the corner of his vision. He felt the pressure of the chair's stuffing against his thighs and buttocks and back and shoulders. His head turned and he found his eyes fixing themselves on the strange incongruity of the empty, clean mustache cup at the end of the table. In the confused turmoil of his sensations, he was mainly aware of the girl's quiet advance and of his own hard breathing. He stood up, made irritable by a consciousness of his own awkwardness, and he said, "What's going on?"

She swayed when she moved; it was an unconscious gracefulness that was part of her at all times. She was so close to him that he could feel the flutter of her breath. She tossed her head back. "You're a good-looking fellow, Charley. I hope your eyes stay clean like that."

"What do you mean?" he said.

"You're fine," she breathed. He felt the soft touch of her fingers, toying with his sleeve, and then when she walked past him he followed her with his eyes. He felt afraid. She went to the kitchen and came back in a minute with a glass half full of red-brown richness. She sipped from it and looked at him with her long eyes over the rim of the glass. Her lips pushed forward thoughtfully and Charley said, "What's on your mind?"

"You."

"What about me?"

"Don't be so damned innocent, Charley. You keep trying to hide behind your age."

"I do?"

"Sometimes you're a little slow, Charley," she suggested.

"Well, maybe I am," he said. Her smile was, he thought, a little sad. He did not understand, but he did not need to. His experience taught him nothing about this moment, and while he tried to think his own feelings betrayed him: he lifted his hands palms-up and displayed great, inarticulate energy, but it was of no avail; he found himself wordlessly encircling the woman's body with his arms. He thrust his face forward and sought her lips. He felt the warm hunger of her mouth, the insistent thrust of her body, and yet, through all of it, there was a nagging corner of his mind that lived through this and was not touched by it except for a dim, faraway regret.

CHAPTER 5

Charley walked slowly down the street to Jim Woods's saloon. The hour was early; the place was almost deserted. Out of his last fifty cents he spent twenty-five on breakfast and the rest, in the course of the morning, on mugs of beer. Norval Douglas

37

did not appear that morning, nor did Jim Woods himself. The wood-frame clock ticked loudly and rang the hours. The bartender told Charley that Woods had taken the mail coach to Stockton to see a man about selling the saloon. No one seemed to know Norval Douglas's whereabouts. Senator Crabb had returned to San Francisco the night before. And, the bartender confided, Chuck Parker was in town.

Mention of Parker's name made Charley's hands become still. It awakened unhappy memories of pain and embarrassment. "Did Parker break out?" he said.

"Released," the barkeep said, stroking his mustache. "Served his time, I guess."

"Hasn't been that long, has it? A year?"

"I don't exactly recall," the barkeep said, and went.

Charley borrowed a pack of cards and played solitaire through the afternoon until at sundown hunger made him impatient with the game and he swept the cards together and turned them in to the bartender. Remembering that there was no money in his pocket, he made friendly talk with the bartender and managed to talk the man into slipping him a few sandwiches. He took one or two more from the tray on the bar when no one was looking, and that was the sum of his supper, consumed quickly in the alley behind the saloon. Afterward he drifted the streets, now and then stopping by Woods's place to find out if Norval Douglas had returned. Someone said he had gone out into the valley to solicit enlistments in Crabb's party. He was expected back any time—but midnight came and went and he did not appear.

Then, on one of his visits to Woods's saloon, Charley caught sight of a massive shape standing far down the bar—Chuck Parker. Charley stood still. The big man stood hipshot, his narrow, suspicious eyes sweeping the crowd with constant wary intensity, and Charley was reminded of the brisk, perfunctory trial that had sent Parker away.

Charley's legs were tired and when a good-natured gambler, flush after a winning streak, offered to buy him a drink, Charley accepted, sitting down at the gambler's table and listening with

38

half his attention to the gambler's talk, which was the idle but insistent talk of a lonely man to whom few people ever listened.

The room was full of hearty people, drinking and smoking in large quantities and talking with loud and friendly ease. At the bar, Chuck Parker was signaling for a cigar and standing with the look of a man quite pleased with himself. His cheeks were round and his body was like a single square-hewn chunk of stone, with vast girths at thighs and waist and chest. His glance surveyed the room with cool detachment, passing over Charley's face without pause or recognition. *Well*, Charley thought, *I guess I've grown a little, changed some*. Parker was regaling a few awe-eyed drunks with stories. At the table with Charley, the lonely gambler kept talking, and Charley listened to him, thinking none of this better than it was. There was a man slumped over a table in a stupor. One of Woods's men just then came to the drunk and pulled him from the chair and boosted him out the door. Thereupon the gambler who had bought Charley's drink said, "Poor Tom. He'll be out in that cold damned street, and he'll tell himself he's cold, but he's not enough of a man any longer to do anything about it. He'll probably die out there unless some kind fool who still has dreams pulls him out of the street and gives him a blanket." And a moment later, smiling coolly, the gambler excused himself politely and left the saloon, apparently to hunt up a blanket. Charley's expression remained blank.

Woods's professor was pounding the battered keys of the spinet, and the rouge-cheeked girls moved around the sawdust floor avoiding the stamping boots of the miners. A *vaquero* came into the place, swept off his huge hat and laughed loudly, afterward making a place at the bar and calling for a drink. Charley wished he was a *vaquero*—they were always laughing.

A husky miner with a pugilistic expression went by, bought a ticket and stood by the rope that defined the limits of the dance floor, waiting his turn. Charley felt in his pocket, and remembered he had no money, and observed that luck was truly indifferent, that you had to endure and reject it with equal sobriety, and that he was hungry again. One o'clock came and went.

39

Chuck Parker was talking to a new group of interested listeners, and Norval Douglas did not appear; Charley remained in the saloon because it was cold and he did not want to sleep in the stable again. His lids were weighted. Men eddied around, trafficked in and out, and gradually the crowd began to diminish and the volume of sound lessened. Chuck Parker shouldered away from the bar and backed against a wall, building a cigarette, covering the room from under the droop of his eyelids. Charley had a good idea of what was on Parker's mind. He watched the big tough with a measure of old contempt in his look. Parker was clearly roving, on the hunt in his animal way, awaiting the passing of some simple prey, and presently Parker's eye fell upon a small hollow-chested old miner who sat eating with his fingers at a table, alone in the back of the place, half drunk or more, with a round-butted leather sack at his elbow—a gold poke. Parker's attention became fixed, and Charley pitied the little drunk miner.

Parker's cheeks were flushed red, broiled to their lobster color by the sun. *Road gang*, Charley thought, seeing the raw marks of chain cuffs on the man's thick wrists. Parker pushed indolently away from the wall and rolled through the crowd out into the night. When Charley looked back, he saw the miner on his feet, swaying a little, pocketing his gold poke. His shoulders were stooped; his beard was ragged. The little man went bent-backed through the place and out the door. Knowing that Parker would soon be upon the miner, Charley, in a fit of accumulated unaimed rage, slipped from his seat and went to the door. He remembered a time when Parker and Bill, the bartender at the Triple Ace, laughing wickedly, had backed him into a corner and hurled obscene insults at him until his face had burned, and with his eyes redly filmed Charley had hurled a chair at Parker and Parker had been too drunk to dodge, so the chair had smashed his face, making his broad flat nose bleed furiously. In unreasoning rage Charley had cried out and Parker had growled and slung his weight forward, trapping Charley in the corner, and had pounded Charley senseless while somewhere in the background Bill was laughing.

That was Charley's memory of Chuck Parker, and now he wheeled out of the saloon doorway and saw the old stooped miner turn a corner two blocks away and fade back into the part of town that consisted mostly of board shacks and tents, where Charley had lived until two days ago. Charley hunched his shoulders against the cold and cursed his thin garments, and quickened his pace as he rounded that corner. He skirted the back of the big mercantile emporium and passed a row of tents and the frame building that was Madam Sarah's, and went up on his toes, running. A wide circle placed him behind a warped, weatherbeaten cabin, where he waited drawing up his breath for the miner to come by so that he could warn the miner against Chuck Parker. Parker would be along soon. Time grew shorter and Charley chafed.

The miner shuffled nearer and lurched against the side of a tent, springing its canvas, speaking to himself in a reasoning way, "On down just a piece more, Ben . . ."

The air had the chill of a sharp knife. The miner came past the edge of the tent, approaching the cabin. The moon was clouded over and it was hard to see anything. Charley was all set to jump out and warn the miner when a huge dark shape loomed in the night and fell upon the old miner, throwing itself upon the man's back, flinging an arm about the miner's neck and a knee into his back; the miner cried out softly, his body arguing ineffectually, and Charley held his breath.

There was a chance. In the shadow of the cabin, Charley stamped his feet, crunching gravel heavily. At that sound of steps, Parker jerked his head up. Charley stamped harder. Parker gave the miner a long shove and whipped about, racing around beyond the tent, soon going beyond earshot.

"Think of that," Charley whispered, a little awed by the effect of his own trick.

The miner was down flat. Charley went to him and knelt. The stillness of the man's body was indication enough that he was dead. There was no pulse, no breath. Charley frowned into the night and cursed Chuck Parker and then, after a moment's thought, slipped the gold poke from the dead miner's pocket.

Afterward, suddenly afraid, he ran through the tent city, legs pumping, halting at last behind the livery barn. In that shadow he waited, trying to calm his breathing. Sometime in the ensuing run of time he heard a man's heavy boots tramp by beyond the stable and he recognized Chuck Parker's steady cursing. A little while thereafter the Negro hostler came out of the side door and shuffled away down the street, and Charley went inside and lay in the straw. The gold poke was heavy in his fist. He put his fingers inside it and sifted the gold dust between his fingers. It was gritty, like sand. He could not be still, and finally he got up and went into the blackness, down to Woods's saloon. He pulled his shoulders together and shoved into the hot stale air of the place. His mind asked tricky questions; he went immediately to the bar. The bartender gave him a curious look and he said, "Norval Douglas been in yet?"

"No," the bartender said. "Hear about the murder?"

"What murder?"

"Ben Crane."

"Who's that?"

"Some old miner. They found his body a while ago."

"Shot?"

"No. Neck broke. Funny thing."

"Yeah," Charley breathed. He looked around. There were very few people in the place. "This Crane—he have a family?" Charley asked.

"Wife and daughter."

"They been told?"

"I guess so," the barkeep said. "Why?"

"No reason, I guess. Where'd he live, this miner?"

"Little shack right behind Cora's place."

"Yeah," Charley said. "Well, I'll see you later." He went out again and stood in the street looking upward. In his pocket his hand toyed with the gold sack. It made his pants sag. The moon was a vague luminescence through the thickness of a cloud whorl. The gambler who earlier had bought a drink for Charley now came down the walk and recognized Charley and touched his hatbrim. Charley said, "You put that fellow to bed?"

"Yes," the gambler said. "I guess this is one more night he'll have to live through," and disappeared into the saloon. Charley pressed his elbows against his sides and looked at the sky again. His feet turned and took him down past the mercantile emporium. The night was very dark and still. A light was on inside the shack behind Cora's crib, and there was the faint sound of weeping through an open window. He felt the taste of despair. Lamplight fell out through that opening and splashed along the earth. A pair of men stood by the door with hats in their hands, and while Charley watched from the shadows those two men spoke softly and soothingly and turned away, putting on their hats and walking away, coming quite close to Charley when they went by, hands in their pockets and heads down. Charley waited until they were gone, then pulled the gold poke from his pocket. He bounced it in his open hand and then raised his arm, and threw the heavy poke overhand. It went through the open window and he heard it strike the floor. There was a small startled cry, a woman's voice. Charley whirled away.

He entered Woods's saloon and went blindly to the bar again. The bartender gave him a questioning glance. Charley felt a hand on his shoulder and almost jumped, and turned to see Norval Douglas's yellow eyes smiling quietly at him. "You're freezing," Douglas said in his gentle drawl. "Let me buy you a drink, boy."

"Obliged." Charley wondered how much the gold poke had been worth. His hand trembled a little when he lifted the drink, and he could not tell if it was from the cold. He nodded to Douglas and then looked past Douglas's shoulder, and his hand tightened on the glass.

Chuck Parker's huge frame filled the doorway, making an aggressive block against the night, and Parker's angry round eyes swept the room. Charley wanted to shrink back, but the bar and Norval Douglas stood there blocking his way. He flinched when Parker's hot glance passed him. Parker mouthed a silent oath and swung away from the door, disappearing into the night. Charley put his back to that and leaned against the rich brown wood of the bar. His hand was unsteady. He said, "All right. Sign me up."

"Fine," Douglas said. He produced a folded piece of paper, opened it and took out a pencil. "Sign here."

"You write it. I'll make my mark."

"Full name?"

"Charles Edward Evans."

"All right," Douglas said, and slid the paper along the bar. "Put your X here."

CHAPTER 6

Giron's belly was soft from many bottles of beer. He stood smoking a cigarette, watching the bearded Pesquiera and the squat, strong Gabilondo. Crests of snow topped the mountains. On the Rio Sonora below, the capital city of Ures lay dusty and quiet. "Once it was Gandara's capital," Pesquiera said. "Now it is ours, eh, Hilario?"

"Sí," Gabilondo murmured. His evil eyes were slitted. Dark, stiff-backed, he stood looking down through the brush.

Giron watched the two of them and felt in his heart certain misgivings. He stood in a mesquite's shadow with his horse's reins in one hand and the other arm braced against a limb of a tree. Clouds like unpicked cotton balls speckled the sky. It was a gentle slope down toward the town, and in the brush below, silent shadows moved—an army of shadows stealing forward upon the unsuspecting capital. Gandara himself had already abandoned the palace. Rumors floated about: Gandara had retreated to the Sierra Madres with the Yaqui Indians to make war on Pesquiera from that stronghold; Gandara had fled to Mexico City to plead with the government for soldiers and aid; Gandara had made his escape by sea to South America; Gandara was dead. No one knew, in truth, where he was. But Giron knew one thing: Gandara was now the *ex*-governor of Sonora.

Gandara had a brother, Jesús, who was more of a fighter than the ex-governor. Jesús Gandara had an adamant army of guerrillas, and it was against these shadow-fighters that Pesquiera's army now moved in the brush below. Jesús Gandara's men still held parts of the town. The action that was about to begin would drive them out, send them into the Sierras where they would have to join their Yaqui allies. Meanwhile, many leagues southward, Benito Juárez was leading his own revolt against Mexico City from the provinces—and Giron was certain that the federal government would be far too busy with Juárez to spare any troops for Gandara. Besides, it was the federal government itself that had denied reappointment to Gandara. At the same time, the government had relieved Gandara's friend Yañez from duty as commanding federal officer in Sonora. Gandara and Yañez were finished; Giron stood satisfied of that. The government had sent Pedro Espejo to replace Yañez as commandante-general, and Espejo—who should arrive shortly—was a friend of Pesquiera's. Further, the government was dispatching one José de Aguilar, who had tried once before and failed to wrest the governorship from Gandara. Now, throughout the territory, Gandara's men were raising the cry that Aguilar and Pesquiera were going to sell the state out to *Norteamericano* filibusters. It was, Giron thought restlessly, very complicated. During Aguilar's previous attempt to seize the governorship, Gandara's deputy had arrested and imprisoned Aguilar. That was what had prompted Pesquiera to take up arms against the governor. During the past summer, on July 17, Pesquiera had besieged the capital here at Ures. On the eighth of August the city had fallen; Pesquiera had released his friend Aguilar from jail, and on the same day Giron had had the satisfaction of routing Gandara's own troops. Altar, Hermosillo, Guaymas—all the cities had slowly yielded to Pesquiera, and today Gandara, wherever he was hiding, was overthrown.

But the ex-governor's brother Jesús still fought. Today it was Giron's mission to guard his general while the troops went into the city and rooted out the guerrillas. By the end of the day, it should be over. Jesús Gandara had but few remaining men.

45

"The attack will begin soon," Pesquiera said. He picked up a knotty twig from the ground and used it to comb his beard. "Giron."

"Sí, general?"

"How many men did you say you have in reserve?"

"Two companies."

"Good. Very good. I am in hopes we will have no need of them."

"I, too."

"We will make use of them if we must," Hilario Gabilondo said, in choppy tones. "Nothing must prevent us from routing the last of them. They are pigs—they must be crushed. We will take the city at any cost."

City. Giron looked down upon the adobe-bounded square, the few narrow streets, the trees of the dusty town. *Gabilondo's glory is all in his head,* he thought. Pesquiera said, "You are too bloodthirsty, Hilario. In due time the last of them will retire. You can see the governor's palace from here, amigos. Tonight we will raise our cups and drink to one another in that palace."

"Sí," Gabilondo said. "Tonight." He eased his muscular squat frame around to consider the sky. "We have made a very successful campaign. Who would have foretold how short it has been?"

"We have been fortunate," Pesquiera said. "I only wish that Manuel Gandara himself were down there in Ures."

Giron thought of him—Don Manuel Gandara. About fifty, he was, of pure Castilian blood, a tall and muscular man. Ruthless, powerful. He owned not only the Topahui grant but eight or nine large *ranchos*, with mines on them. Truly, he was a despot—now to be deposed.

"It is my feeling," Gabilondo said stiffly, "that Gandara is back in the mountains with his Yaqui friends. Friends—bah. I pray soon he will find out just what kind of friends he has bought for himself. The Yaquis will give him little enough support, once they find his power has been crushed. *Mi general,* I would like your leave to lead a party into the Sierra Madres. I will cut them to pieces and bring Gandara's head to you."

Pesquiera waved a hand flutteringly, lazily. "You are too impatient, Hilario. Your thirst for death is too anxious. There is time for everything—and if you hope to outwit the Yaquis in their own stronghold, then you are not as wise a man as I had thought."

Giron listened to this conversation while his eyes remained on the flitting shadows in the brush below. Soon those shadows would achieve the rim of the flats. Giron observed, with some soldierly contempt, that if he were Gabilondo, then he personally would be down there to lead the troops. It was a general's place. But no; Gabilondo sat here safe on the hillside. Behind the hill waited Giron's reserve force of two companies—peons, volunteers. Well armed, they were, with the *Norteamericanos'* guns; but Giron had his doubts about their courage, their marksmanship, their fighting ability. He blinked. Ah, well; a man could but do with what he had.

Gabilondo's head jerked up. "*Leche*," he swore. "*Chingado*. The fools are too close to the open—they will expose themselves. *Cabrones!*" Gabilondo strode away, leading his horse, mounting up when he had achieved the concealment of the tall brush.

Giron stood alone on the hillside then with Pesquiera, and Pesquiera said in a tone of dry amusement, "One would think that Gabilondo was mapping a vast campaign, instead of a small action. Ah—here comes our new governor." He turned, sweeping off his hat.

Riding down between the mesquites and manzanitas was a diminutive man, point-bearded, bright of eye—José de Aguilar. Aguilar was to act as figurehead governor. It was, Giron knew, a temporary state of affairs meant to placate the government at Mexico City; in time Aguilar would be quietly disposed of and Pesquiera himself would step into his place.

But Aguilar, knowing none of this, rode forward with the proud bearing of a leader. Dismounting, he handed his reins to Giron and turned to Pesquiera, showing him no more than the deference a man shows his hireling. "Here you are, my friend." Pesquiera only smiled slightly and bowed with exact courtesy. "Welcome," he said softly. "From this gallery, my governor, you shall watch the last act unfold in our little revolutionary drama."

47

And Pesquiera, eyes a-twinkle, swept his arm off toward Ures, quiet in the sunlit valley. Giron, made uncertain and dour by intrigues, only watched expressionlessly. Downhill there was a horseman's hat bobbing forward through the brush, Hilario Gabilondo's hat. Gabilondo reached the edge of the open flats, lifted his hat and leaned forward in the saddle, galloping out toward town. Giron felt mild surprise to see Gabilondo actually leading the attack.

It was farcical; even Giron, loyal as he was, had to admit that. A few puffs of white powdersmoke went up from the town walls, followed a short time later by the distant crack of musketry. Gabilondo's regiment assaulted the adobe walls, swept over them and drove through the streets of Ures. There was very little shooting.

"A simplicity," Pesquiera said fifteen minutes later, when tiny figures on the distant town plaza were seen herding prisoners together. "Gabilondo's great charge," Pesquiera murmured, and laughed low in his throat. "Governor?"

"Yes?" said Aguilar.

"I trust you did not forget to dispatch a man to San Francisco."

"To General Cosby," Aguilar said, and smiled complacently. "I did not forget, old friend. One of my best men left by sea four days ago from Port Lobos."

"Good," Pesquiera said. "It might prove embarrassing to have Cosby crawling up behind us with his proposed thousand-man filibustering army." He turned to Aguilar and grinned, touching the small man's pointed shoulder. "We must have none of that, eh, Governor?"

"None of that," Aguilar echoed mildly, and Giron, frowning, wondered what it was they were talking of.

CHAPTER 7

On the twenty-first of January, Charley boarded the *Sea Bird* at its San Francisco wharf. He was early for sailing; the others had not yet arrived. Black water lapped at the gunwales and the sidewheels; the ship rubbed gently against the dock, and the gangplank swayed and bowed under his weight when he went up, hauling his carpetbag and rifle and the new overcoat his advance wages had bought him. The carpetbag was heavy with the weight of a Navy Colt revolver and its accoutrements—bullets, mould, powder flask, percussion caps, cleaning gear.

He made his way to the sleeping quarters below decks and stowed his gear there, carpetbag and rifle, underneath a swaying hammock. This steerage hold was like a long low-roofed dormitory, with flat bulkheads fore and aft, and precious little light admitted by the spotted portholes. It was a bleak, windy Wednesday and now, at seven in the morning, the fog was beginning to clear off the bay. He went to a porthole and looked through at the teeming streets of the town. A Chinese with vast sleeves stood by the open tailgate of a wagon, hawking souvenirs at the dock entrance, his hair tied back in a pigtail. The town sloped up precariously from the wharves. Two large Negroes tooled a heavy freight wagon onto the dock and cables came down from the deck above, hooking onto the cargo.

The packet would not begin to board the Crabb party for half an hour yet. The quiet was unsettling. Charley took a turn up through the hatch and hauled out onto the deck for a breath of harbor air. Seamen were busy fitting cargo into a forward hold. The captain, a tubercular-looking figure in a shapeless greatcoat and seagoing cap, stood up on the Texas deck, arms akimbo, watching the activity. Charley saw Market Street angling up through the wooden town, and absently watched the busy early-morning traffic on that thoroughfare as he huddled

inside his heavy coat against the cutting chill of the harbor. A
sailor with his hat at a jaunty angle came rolling by and grinned
at him and went on to the cargo hoist. An overturned lifeboat
was lashed at the rail, hung on a skyhook harness. He walked
around the hardwood decking, admired the teak trim of the
Texas ramp, and presently found himself in the saloon.

He stood aside from the door to look the place over. For a
steam packet, it was a large room, characterized by a worn
scarlet carpet and massive crystal chandeliers and scattered,
green-felt gaming tables. It was vaguely reminiscent of the in-
terior of Jim Woods's place, but the bar was at the wrong end of
the room; otherwise the resemblance would have been striking
—and Charley wondered if Woods hadn't patterned his place
after some such shipboard room.

Only the bartender was present, arranging his stock behind
the knurled-edge bar. Charley moved forward and took a cup of
steaming strong coffee, borrowed a pack of cards and set up his
solitaire game at a table. Solitaire was a good game. It kept
your hands busy. Red ten on black jack. Red and black—he recalled his stepfather's maroon shirts, brought West from Creole
haunts, his black pegged trousers so out-of-place on a farm, his
black-leather Bible and the red-amber shine of his whisky bottle,
always near at hand.

In an hour the boat was filled with a crowd. Charley was on
deck once more, at the rail. The captain was shouting down
from his pilot house over the Texas deck. The teamsters on the
dock made way for a hansom, and Charley saw two men step
down: Henry Crabb and a Mexican, probably Crabb's brother-
in-law, Sus Ainsa. Crabb turned and a dark, slight woman
emerged from the cab on his arm. Crabb leaned forward and
planted a gentle kiss on the woman's lips. She was dressed in
black, which made her appear very small and fragile. Crabb
touched her cheek with a finger and the woman got back into
the cab. Then he whipped his arm up and the cab driver nodded
and began backing the horses to turn around; Crabb stood on
the wharf until the cab went from sight up the cobblestone
street. Two men in livery were carrying luggage on board, and

presently Crabb and his brother-in-law came up the ramp. Ainsa was lanky and darkly handsome; he moved in a loose-jointed manner and had an easy smile. Those two men went directly around into Crabb's cabin suite. From overhead, the captain shouted: "Haul in the planks!"

The forward plank was drawn up and the crew converged aft to pull in that gangplank. A crowd of men rushed onto the wharf and one of them bawled, "Leave that Goddamn plank down!"

Charley recognized Chuck Parker and Bill Randolph in that crowd, a roistering loud bunch of burly men. The crewmen looked at one another with uncertainty; a man detached himself from that group and moved toward the upper deck, where the captain and pilot stood watching. But by then, Bill and Parker and the others were on board, grinning derisively at the crewmen. "All right," Bill said. "You can haul it in now." Laughing, he slapped a sailor on the back and wheeled forward with his retinue, a filthy mass of men smelling of whisky and body stink, hauling miscellaneous duffelbags and luggage, dressed in rumpled clothing.

The plank wheeled in; lines were cast off and presently the boat got underway, wheels churning, smoke lifting in a back-tilted gray column from the stack. When they steamed through the Golden Gate, Charley was at the rail near the bow, and saw the cannon emplacements of Fort Scott looming high overhead in the thin mist. The air had a flesh-biting cold in it and, huddling inside his heavy new coat, Charley went below, and found Norval Douglas savoring the taste of a cigar in the saloon.

The room had filled quickly. Charley leaned back against the bar. Douglas was observing the room's bustling activity with bemused tolerance. Above the high curve of his cheekbones his eyes burned and glowed. Charley saw the fighting streak along his friend's mouth and had the feeling that, if the mood moved Douglas, he would kill with deliberate coolness. His face, square at the jawbone, was handsome and sure; deviltry, planned or remembered, sparked in his eyes. He wore a clean brown cotton shirt and butternut trousers, and a belted Navy pistol.

A voice beside Charley said, "Whisky." Douglas looked past

Charley at that man. Charley had never seen him before; it was a tall blond man, round-faced, who turned a flashing German smile on Douglas and said, "We've met before, I think."

"I was with William Walker," Douglas said, extending his hand.

"Ah—that's right. I'm Zimmerman. Correspondent for the New York *Times*." He turned and swept the room with easy eyes. "A drink?"

"All right," Douglas said, and introduced Charley to the man.

Zimmerman with his German smile said, "A drink, son?" and Charley shook his head. "I'll take coffee."

"Well enough," said Zimmerman. "Two whiskies and a coffee, bartender."

Norval Douglas leaned back against the bar, hooking his thumbs idly in his gunbelt and letting his drink stand when it came.

"You're with Crabb, I presume," Zimmerman said.

"Is there anyone on this boat who's not with Crabb?" Charley said.

"I don't suppose so. No one but myself and my sister." Zimmerman pulled out a pad and began to scribble with the stub of a pencil, making corrections in something he had written there. He spoke abstractedly while he wrote. "I'm always curious to know what sparks a man to join an expedition of this kind. Is it the promise of adventure?"

"Not particularly," Douglas murmured.

"Money, then."

"Why, I wouldn't say that."

"Just seeing what's over the hill," Zimmerman suggested, not looking up from his pencil work.

"That's close enough," Douglas said. His eyes appeared sleepy. "I've seen the hills before, but sometimes I get the feeling I must have missed something the first time."

"You might say you were looking for answers," Zimmerman said.

That was all well enough, Charley noticed, but before you found the answers you had to know what kind of questions to ask. He watched the brown-amber swirl of Zimmerman's drink as he gently turned the glass. The correspondent nodded over his notebook and pushed it along the bar toward Douglas. "See what you think of that."

Douglas perched the cigar between his teeth, glanced at Charley, and began to read aloud:

"To the *Times*. I am enabled through the courtesy of one of General Crabb's staff, to forward you the following list of the officers of the great Arizona Colonization Company." His eyes lifted. "Arizona, Mr. Zimmerman?"

"According to your Captain McKinney," Zimmerman said, and added drily, "He seems to feel that Sonora will be a part of Arizona before long."

Douglas gave Charley a dour glance and went on reading: "Their combined force is said to amount to fifteen hundred men on this coast, with large additions to arrive from Texas, under command of officers regularly appointed." Douglas shook his head wryly. "There are ninety of us on this boat. Not fifteen hundred."

"The rest will follow. I have it on the captain's assurance."

"Good for him," Douglas murmured. He skipped over the officer list and read another page from the notebook: "At present the organization appears only as a party of peaceful emigrants combining to resist Indian attack. I understand that its leaders intend to preserve this character and not to violate any United States statute until every arrangement is complete, when they will cross the line and with their allies in Sonora make their issue open and in strong force. Signed, 'Z'." Douglas handed the notebook back. "Good enough, I suppose. Why ask me? I'm not an officer."

"That's exactly why I did ask you. Tell me, what precisely is your position?"

"Scout and guide," Douglas said. "I've been over the ground before."

"Yes. With William Walker." Smiling his round-cheeked smile, Zimmerman pocketed the notebook and pushed away. "I'll see you gentlemen later."

"Obliged for the coffee," Charley said. He caught the correspondent's nod and watched him leave. Norval Douglas said, "I wonder what he gets out of this kind of thing?" and left the bar too, leaving Charley alone with his coffee. It was amazing, he observed, how little anyone could know about anyone else. The coffee had cooled down and he sipped at its tepid strength. In a far part of the saloon he saw two large figures—Bill Randolph and Chuck Parker. A crowd of recent memories washed through him and in a moment he found himself thinking of Gail with a strange mixture of compassion and anger. The pale light from windows and chandeliers made a flat, almost vapid choleric unhealthiness of everyone's flesh. Charley retreated in stiff silence from the room.

There was no one below decks. He stood by his hammock and after a moment dragged out his carpetbag. The men in the saloon, he had noticed, were most of them armed. He tugged the belted revolver out of the bag, strapped the holster on, and held the gun in his hand, balancing its unfamiliar weight. The long octagonal barrel was crisp and smooth and straight; there was something clean and positive about it. He loaded it methodically. Dropping the hammer between two chambers, he hefted the gun and found it heavier than it had been. The weight of armed power amplified the two-and-a-half pounds of the gun. He slid his palm over the smooth hardwood grip and balanced the barrel over his crooked elbow, taking aim at a porthole, squinting with one eye over the tiny brass bead of the front sight. He imagined enemies balanced over that sight—Indians, breechclouted, leaping; Mexicans in battle dress; Bill Randolph in a soiled white apron. He pulled the trigger. The hammer was down; nothing happened; but in his imagination he felt the hard kick against his palm and saw the drift of clouded powdersmoke and the pitching of his stricken enemy. His eyes grew wide in the musty dimness of the hold. He holstered the gun and buttoned the flap over it, and went up the ladder with his shoulders straight and his eyes level and half-shuttered, in imitation of Norval Douglas.

The *Sea Bird* swayed gently, paddlewheels thrumming the

water. Smoke columned behind them like a trailing flag. The colors of the ocean were gray and green and brown-blue, with now and then a fleck of white toward the distant coastline. That shore was a ragged uplift of rocks and sharp-sloping timber, gnarled flatheaded cypresses and oak.

There was a man on deck at the rail. He offered Charley a cigar, then lit his own pipe and introduced himself: "My name is John Edmonson." He spoke in carefully modulated tones, precisely pronounced; he seemed to be an educated man from far away. His cheeks were stubbled with gray, his lean face deeply lined. He had a long straight nose and mild eyes that made him appear gentle and thoughtful; there were two horse-pistols in his waistband. He appeared old. He said, "Have you ever stopped to wonder about the sea? I wonder what might be hidden underneath that surface. A good many mysteries, I suspect."

"Sharks," Charley said. "And stingrays."

"I should have thought," Edmonson murmured, "that a youth like yourself would have plenty of time yet to turn into a cynic."

"Into what?"

"A cynic," the older man said, "is a man who believes the worst of everything—and by the same token, believes in nothing."

Charley thought that was a fairly accurate description of himself. He saw nothing wrong with it; life came to him that way, in hues of black and gray. He spoke with customary bluntness: "You seem a little tame for this war party."

"Perhaps I am. Perhaps a few tame old men are needed among us."

"It's bound to be a hard trip."

"My bones aren't so old yet that I can't ride horseback," Edmonson said with a friendly smile. His voice was a gentle husky buzz. Under the rim of his flat-crowned California hat his hair stuck out in unruly licks of pebbled gray. He was tall, not bent. The sea traveled past without changing. "I feel the need for lunch," Edmonson said. "Join me?"

"All right."

Over the meal, the old man talked mildly of remembered things. He was a New Englander, and his nostalgic conversation evoked in Charley's mind fanciful pictures of places he had never seen. Edmonson's family, once wealthy enough to educate him, had seen the coin turn; his father, he said, had gone bankrupt and died soon after. Edmonson revealed that he had studied for the law, but ill health in the form of lung consumption had driven him West. His body had healed. The need to earn a living had kept him at the carpenter's trade; thus the calluses on his palms. He had never owned the talent for accumulating money. Approaching age had turned his thoughts toward a home, and Crabb had promised that—land on which to settle. He said, "I believe the prospects of danger are not nearly so great as some of us would believe. And where men will build homes, they will have need of a carpenter. I've found it a satisfying livelihood."

"Is that all you want out of it?" Charley asked.

"What do you mean?"

"I don't know," Charley said. "It just seems to me there ought to be something more than just making a living with your hands."

"It's more than sufficient to keep a man content. To demand more out of life is to delude yourself. In time you may learn that, my young friend."

"Maybe."

"What more would you have out of life?"

Charley would have to consider that. He made no immediate answer. After a while Edmonson said, "There's another young man aboard, about your age. His name is Chapin. I found him singularly uncommunicative. Have you met him?"

"No."

"I'll be curious to see what you make of him."

"All right," Charley said absently. He felt no particular interest. Presently he finished his meal and left Edmonson to his pipe, and walked once more onto the deck.

During the afternoon he spent an hour watching a dice game in the steerage, visited the engine room and stood deafened by the thump and hiss of the great pistons and watched the stokers move steadily with their shovels, men with glistening torsos and massive arms. Afterward he moved restlessly about the ship. Twilight came in shifting layers over the sea and the *Sea Bird* rocked gently, big paddlewheels churning, engines thrumming. The coastline was somewhere out of sight off the port side. A brittle cold wind came off the ocean but Charley stood fast in the twilight after supper, holding the rail with numb fingers and staring into the darkening colors of the sea. He was beginning to know the fear of uncertainty: Why had he come?

Violet and cobalt dusk, and up above on the Texas deck someone lighted collision lanterns. Silence enveloped Charley. His face, long and spare of lips, grew sharp, reserved, bitter.

After a stretch of time gray Jim Woods came up from below decks, made one turn about the rail, remarked to Charley about the cold, and went back inside. A crewman came along checking the lifeboat lashings; storm clouds were visible in the southwest. Overhead the captain came out of the wheelhouse and stood with the wind in his face, rubbing his arms. A cabin door opened a little way down the deck and he watched the correspondent, Zimmerman, leave that stateroom and come down the deck toward him. As Zimmerman passed alongside, Charley said, "Evening."

Zimmerman started. He looked into the shadows. "Oh—hello, Evans," he muttered, and went down the stairwell into the saloon.

Charley frowned. His eyes put themselves on the lighted glass of the wheelhouse; the captain turned back inside after shooting the sky with a sextant. The door beyond Zimmerman's stateroom opened and Charley was surprised to see a woman's shape emerge—no, it was a girl's. The girl came forward and Charley bit his lip—she seemed to bear a strange resemblance to Gail. Her hair was tawny. He stepped out of the lifeboat's shadow, startling her, and introduced himself, using Zimmerman's name; he said, "He told us he had a sister on board. You'd be Miss Zimmerman?"

"Why," she said, "yes."

"Going for a walk on deck, ma'am?"

"Yes, I was." Her voice and expression were uncertain.

57

He stepped back. "I'm sorry. I didn't mean to bother you."

She nodded and went on; a short time later she reappeared at the far end of the deck, having made a circuit of the boat, and he watched her come forward. He expected her to go back into her cabin, but she did not. She came on and said to him, "You look half frozen."

"I'll go below. There's a stove in the saloon."

"No," she said abruptly. "Come with me—get dry by the stove. Really, you must." She turned about and walked back to her cabin, and turned again to see if he was following. Frowning, alert but unsure, he went after her and stopped in the door, looking down. "I didn't mean to bother you."

The girl reached forward and pulled him gently inside, closing the door behind him. Her smile was open and frank; but it went away suddenly and she blushed. "I wonder what made me do that?"

She was, he guessed, not much older than he was. "You're shivering," she said, and moved him toward the little round stove in the room's corner. Its isinglass window glared redly. "Take off your coat," she said. "Why, you're soaked with spray. How long were you on deck?"

"Longer than I thought." He shouldered out of his coat and stood bent over the stove, welcoming its warmth. "I'm always doing stupid things like that."

"What's your name?"

"Charley Evans."

"I'm Helen."

"Hello," he said; his back was still to her, but now he turned to warm his legs and buttocks, and lifted his hand to sweep damp hair out of his eyes. The girl said, "I suppose you shouldn't be here with the door closed."

"You're right. I'd better go."

"No," she said. "You'll freeze if you go out again. Besides, my brother keeps busy with his interviews and I have no one for company. I like having someone to talk to."

"Why," he said, "so do I."

"There can't be anything wrong with that," she said firmly,

and glanced at the closed door. Lamplight cast shadows under her brows; he could not make out the color of her eyes. Her face was oval and pleasant. She wore a long brown skirt and a white waist. He saw rising interest in her eyes; he let himself smile.

CHAPTER 8

"After that," Charley said, "I took on Ed's chores. He was six years older then, so naturally he was a lot bigger—it about broke my back at first, but after a while I learned how to handle everything. The old man didn't do much but drink, and my mother quit talking altogether. The place got pretty run down, because I couldn't keep it up all by myself, and the old man didn't do much work at all, he just went back to his Bible and his bottle, and I got to figuring that I didn't have an old man at all—just an old drunk I had to support. I packed up and left when I was thirteen. The old man was pretty bad off with the whisky sickness."

"What happened to them?" the girl said.

"It doesn't much matter, does it? Maybe they're still on the same old farm, him drinking and her crying." He stopped quickly. How had she drawn him out? He remembered Gail and he regretted having confided in this woman.

Her lips were pursed; she looked up in a faraway manner. "What have you done since then?"

He shrugged. "Worked. Odd jobs, town to town."

"It makes my life sound so sheltered and dreary," she said.

Lamplight flickered across his face frostily. His lips were pressed together. He didn't want to talk more about himself. "What about you?" he said. "What are you doing on this boat?"

"Our parents died last month," she told him. "There was nowhere else to go. My brother brought me with him. I'm taking the *Sea Bird* around to the East. I'll go to school, I suppose."

"How old are you?"

"Seventeen."

"I'm eighteen," he lied. He picked up his coat from the bunk and held it near the fire to dry it out; he aimed a slantwise look at the girl and saw color come slowly to her cheeks. Her hair fell carelessly about her shoulders and a smile lay in suggestion behind the composure of her lips. Her body was rounded, a little heavy, and sight of it fed his desires. "Maybe I'd better get below," he said.

"Stay just a little longer."

She was neither a whore nor a barmaid. He gave her a quiet stare and moved toward the door, sliding his arm into the coat. The girl, sitting on her bunk, threw her head back so that he could see the throbbing of her throat and the pale blue of her eyes. When he opened the door a frigid wind met him in the face. He said, "Maybe I'll see you tomorrow."

"Yes."

"Thanks for listening."

"I liked it."

He went out, pulling the door shut behind him. Light beads of sweat were cold on his forehead. He stood just outside the door, hand on the latch, watching the dappled surface of the moon and the glistening reflections of the sea; the engines rumbled and the packet's deck swayed with the motion of the seas, and a man's figure came up from the saloon—Zimmerman. Obviously recognizing Charley, he advanced with a swelling rush and said angrily, "What were you doing in there?"

"Talking. Thawing out."

"Hell," Zimmerman said. His smooth round cheeks were dark. He moved in on Charley stiff-armed. The blow caught Charley under the heart and staggered him; he found himself falling across the deck into the rail. Instantly there was rage; he came back, swinging clumsy round blows toward Zimmerman and smelling the stink of whisky on the correspondent's breath—his fist hauled up from the waist and cracked Zimmerman's lips; and that was all.

It amazed him. Zimmerman fell back with a dull sound against the cabin wall, and stood there dazed, fingering his jaw. His free hand waggled and he said, "All right—all right. Enough." He worked his jaw back and forth with his hand. The door opened and the girl was outlined there, talking quickly, asking questions which no one answered. Zimmerman said, "Sorry, Evans. I was drunk. No hard feelings?"

"No," Charley said, "I guess not." He looked into the girl's eyes and saw puzzlement there; he turned his collar up and went away, amazed by how easy it was to get the better of some men.

Restless and warmed by exertion, he made a tour around the deck and went below. He picked his way past card games and sleeping drunks to his hammock, and took some time getting used to the bent swaying position he had to assume; then he was asleep quickly.

Rough seas wakened him at four in the morning, and he spoke a number of oaths while untangling himself from the swinging hammock. Several lurching men staggered toward the rear bulkhead, looking very sick in the weird lunging light thrown by the swinging lamps. Someone threw the bulkhead door open and the line of green-faced men plunged through toward the ladder. Charley swore again and braced himself against a post. Nearby a loose-hanging lantern heaved back and forth, and had the effect of upsetting his balance by constantly shifting the shadows. Men were shouting and bodies rolled past him in what seemed to be aimless directions. Sea smell was strong. A little pool of water moved back and forth near his feet. Old John Edmonson came by with a sickly smile, said, "I don't believe I was cut out for this," and made his way to the ladder. Across the room, Charley saw Norval Douglas and Jim Woods give up their attempt to continue a card game. Two or three men came back down from topside, very pale, and one of them said, "It's worse up there. The damned boat's upside down." Over it all was the smash of water against the decks and the steady imperturbable thrum of the engines.

A man Charley knew from Tuolumne County, Sam Kimmel, rocked past him and bumped into the massive lurching body of

Chuck Parker, and Sam Kimmel stopped abruptly, wiping his lips. "Here you are, you son of a bitch."

Parker wheeled ponderously. "What?"

"I've been looking for you."

Men were cursing and wheeling about the cabin. Kimmel stood fast, a small one-eyed man with an embittered expression, stubbornly ignoring the ship's vast movements; Kimmel said in precisely enunciated words, "You Goddamned son of a bitch. I figured to catch up to you one day, you thieving bastard."

Charley watched with mixed fascination and fear. Parker's hot round eyes sizzled against Kimmel. The lamps whirled and shadows danced. The boat's bottom struck a trough of water, jarring everyone loose, and Charley pitched down the steeply sloping floor until the bulkhead stopped him hard. When he looked back he saw an intertwined crawling mass that slowly took shape and became eyes and arms and legs. Out of that confusion stepped Norval Douglas. He braced himself against the wall by a porthole. The boat rolled over and the mass of bodies separated. Chuck Parker was still rooted by his hammock. His face was distorted with wrath; he bore down mightily upon the slight form of Samuel Kimmel, and then Kimmel pulled a pocket-pistol from somewhere and trained it uncertainly on Parker and shouted above the din of sea and storm: "You've got this coming to you, damn you!" Parker stopped in his tracks and Norval Douglas pushed forward, palming his own revolver. Once again the waves parted and the ship plunged downward, heeled over. Charley scratched for a grip. Dimly he heard the report of a gunshot, and when the boat slowly righted itself he saw Chuck Parker with one leg buckling under him, dropping to the deck. He lifted himself to one elbow and looked down and said, in a stupid voice, "You put a slug in my leg. What for?"

Kimmel stumbled forward and knelt by him. His single fevered eye peered at the injured leg. "Jesus. I didn't really mean to pull the Goddamn trigger."

Parker's sluggish features turned petulant. He glared at the black eyepatch. Kimmel said, "I'm sorry"—Charley saw his lips form the words. Norval Douglas was leaning down over Parker. Kimmel got up. "I'll find Dr. Oxley. Stay put, Parker."

"I ain't going anywhere," Parker said. "You son of a bitch. I don't even know you. What the hell did you do that for?"

"You cheated me in a card game," Kimmel said, and the whole thing appeared silly to Charley.

Men were getting sick all over the big cabin and the stench became bad. Kimmel disappeared, on the hunt for Oxley, the surgeon. Parker lay regarding his wounded leg with undiminished surprise. His lips worked together. Norval Douglas knelt to press a handkerchief against the wound and stem the bleeding. The smell of vomit in the room drove Charley to his feet. He put his coat on and went stumbling to the ladder, and climbed out of the cabin.

Coming on deck, he stood aside to let the doctor rush past, and looked out upon a heavy ocean. The clumsy packet, bracing the wind, fell into a trough, and Charley fell across the deck against the railing. When he pulled himself up he saw a lantern break loose and fall flaming to the decks. The ship pitched over and the lamp rolled down the slanting deck to be lost in the sea. High spray extinguished the sparks left behind. A man, trying to tighten some ropes, rolled off balance and ran yelling down the ship. Doors slammed and cabins emptied their occupants into the night. The *Sea Bird* wheeled ponderously over onto a precarious keel, and a cargo hoist abruptly broke loose and dropped into the cabin wall. There was a high sound of crushing wood, and then while the captain and mates came out on deck to observe the damage, the ship went over once more and the hoist slid back, smashing through the starboard rail and rolling into the ocean, immediately disappearing in foam.

The captain scaled the rigging and bawled, "Helmsman— helmsman—keep her into the wind, God damn it!" Figures came and went on the slippery deck. A freak turn of wind brought an unseen crewman's voice to Charley's ears: "Raise her up, now. Heave!" The ship bumped rock-hard water and the captain slipped from the rigging and landed hard on the tilted deck; he slid down the deck to the shattered cabin wall and pulled himself back from that and reeled toward the Texas ladder. When he came by, Charley heard him talking to himself in loud and angry terms: "I'll keelhaul the man responsible for securing that hoist." And went on up to the pilot house.

The saloon door batted open and two men—Crabb and Sus Ainsa—were outlined in the dizzy light; the door slammed shut. Helen Zimmerman came out of her cabin with a heavy coat over her dressing gown and screamed when the ship rolled. She fell to the deck, climbed to her feet and windmilled wildly to regain balance, trying to get back to her cabin. The ship went over still a few more degrees, and the girl slid across the deck against the rail, grabbing hold. Still heeling over, the ship maintained a precarious equilibrium against the port beam, and a wheeling spar spun along the mainmast to knock a heavy pole down. The pole skidded across the deck and Charley saw it lodge against the girl. On that sign Charley let go his hold and half-slid, half-fell down across the deck to the girl. He lifted the heavy wood off her and saw it drop into the hungry sea. For a moment he was staring horizontally into the whiteness of the ocean. The girl moaned and grasped him in a locked grip about the waist. Charley took her at the shoulders as the ship plunged into another trough. Slate-colored sheets of water swept the decks madly. The mate came into sight crazily lurching and bawling obscenities into the night, and lost his balance, falling against the rail and teetering on it for a long time; the boat lifted its side and the mate slowly tumbled over backwards, sliding across the slick deck and disappearing down an open hatch. He screamed as he went out of sight.

A whirling mass of men surrounded the braces of the starboard lifeboat, and when Charley noticed them they were trying to lower the boat. Some fool cut the cables, and the water lifted massively and came down all confusion over the freed lifeboat, capsizing it. The crowd backed up in horror, moaning loudly, and the captain shouted hoarsely from the Texas deck: "Get inside, you idiots!"

The girl spoke against his chest; Charley could not make out her words. He saw the bodies of struggling people battered about

64

on the storm-tossed deck, and then a great plunging mass of water shattered over his head.

Breaking over him, the force of the sea tore loose his hold on the rail. He heard a scream. The water carried him away from the deck and he had the awful sensation that he was going to drown. He felt the girl's hands hooked into his belt. The sea slammed them down onto the deck, whirled them about, pulled greedily at them; they bobbed and flattened against the ship. The foam rippled away leaving the deck high-sloping in the air. Head hanging down, Charley gasped in gulps of air and spray. He saw the girl lying across the deck and, beyond her, the eerie whiteness of a man's face, the correspondent, her brother. Zimmerman grinned widely at him and shouted, "Hang on!" And just as Charley sought a handhold the water swept over them.

He lurched about and when the water receded again he could not lift his head to see the sky, but he knew by the gray light reflected from the deck that the dawn was coming up somewhere; he could see only the ocean and the glistening deck. The boat dropped stern-first. His hands were locked on a hatch wheel. Charley pulled in his breath. His legs were numb. The sea flashed over them again, impetuously angry but now in retreat, and when its fingers slid away he looked at the corpse-hue of Zimmerman's face and the dead-stubborn way Zimmerman was hanging on to his sister, and Charley wondered how it was that a man could give up a fist fight so easily and yet brave a storm at sea with level courage.

The *Sea Bird* plunged up and down. Charley's nose hit the deck. He felt the warmth of blood in his nostrils and heard the muffled run of his own oaths. Zimmerman's voice shouted faintly across the few feet between them:

"Let's try and get inside."

"Go ahead," Charley said, forcing his tongue to form words.

"Can you make it?"

"I don't know if my legs will work. Go on—go on."

"Jesus," Zimmerman shouted, "I hate heroes. Come on, Evans."

He felt the correspondent's hand tight on his arm and saw Zimmerman's other hand supporting the girl; he threw all his concentration into climbing onto the precarious stilts of his legs and hobbling on them across the swinging deck. Gray sleet pummeled his cheeks; the world rocked underfoot and water dashed the boat with massed energy.

CHAPTER 9

The *Sea Bird* swayed deliberately. He found himself drifting fitfully into aimless dreams. There was a vast bright desert and a single staggering form, and he was thirsty; there was a high forest and the bounding white haunches of an antelope. Then it was dark, and the spray came over him, and water lapped at his feet on a beach somewhere.

A hand touched his arm and he sat bolt upright.

"Bad dreams?" Zimmerman said.

"Not so bad." Charley blinked, finding himself on Zimmerman's bunk, naked and wrapped in a blanket. Zimmerman stood by the stove holding Charley's coat toward the heat, standing with feet braced wide against the ship's heavy rolling. The storm, apparently, had dissipated. "Your sister all right?" Charley said.

"Yes, she's fine. In her cabin. We owe you a lot of thanks for getting that spar off her—she might have been knocked overboard."

Sunlight came in through the open port. Zimmerman swayed slowly back and forth with the motion of the floor. "How do your legs feel?"

Charley moved his legs. "All right. What time is it?"

"Noon. I guess you're hungry."

"I guess I am," Charley said. "Thanks for putting me up."

"Your clothes are dry. Let's go down and get something to eat—if the food wasn't washed overboard."

"Did we lose anybody in the weather?"

"Not that I know of."

"Lucky," Charley said, and climbed out of bed.

"One of the sailors got a bump on the head from falling through a hatch. And one of your men—Parker—was shot accidentally in the leg last night."

"I know." Charley felt no particular pity for Chuck Parker. As Kimmel, who had shot him, had said, Parker had it coming.

His expression was dour when he followed Zimmerman into the mess hall. The room was crowded with a noon-meal crowd. At the captain's table sat General Crabb and Sus Ainsa and the officers. Charley recognized Oxley, the surgeon, and Captains McDowell, Holliday, and McKinney. There were half a dozen other officers whose names he did not know. Charley had seen most of them only at a distance.

Norval Douglas and Jim Woods sat at the first officer's table. That was where Zimmerman and Charley sat down. A heated conversation was in progress; Woods was talking: "—you can settle it, Norval. You were with the Walker expedition in 'Fifty-four."

"It was a bloody mess," Douglas said imperturbably. His eyes acknowledged Charley's presence.

"There," said Woods. "You see? None of them are easy, O'Rouke."

O'Rouke, a commonplace man with a ragged beard, said, "Just the same, this is different. We're going down there to protect them, not invade them."

"It will be fine," Woods said, "if the Mexicans see it the same way you do. Hell, do you think we'd be gettin' such high pay if we wasn't going to be taking risks?"

"We haven't been paid so high yet," Charley said.

Woods turned a mock-angry glance on him. "Leave that kind of talk be," he said with a friendly tone. "There's always one joker like you in the crowd, Charley. You're a God-awful pessimist."

"What I see makes me that way," Charley said, and bit into his meal.

67

The conversation continued between Woods and O'Rouke. Norval Douglas paid little attention to it. After a while his yellow eyes came around to Charley and he said, "I understand you did a nice piece of work last night. Didn't get hurt, did you?"

"No."

"That was a mean blow."

"I hope I don't see another one like it," Zimmerman said.

"We lost a cargo hoist," Woods put in. "That'll make unloading pretty slow at the dock tomorrow."

"There's no hurry," Douglas said, and got up to leave, a toothpick in hand. His lean form ambled out of the room and soon the tables emptied.

When he came out on deck into the warming sun of the early afternoon, Charley found a youth lounging at the rail. He remembered that old John Edmonson had told him there was another young man in the party; restless, Charley went toward the youth, who was tall and very thin with tousled dark hair and an underslung chin. Charley said, "You in the Crabb outfit?"

The youth gave him a stare of evident discomposure and said nervously, "Yes—yes." His eyes were fever-bright.

"I'm Charley Evans."

"Carl Chapin." The thin youth accepted Charley's handshake and once more turned his troubled glance out to sea. Out there he seemed to be seeing the darkness of his own future. The paddlewheels churned with steady grunts and regular splashes. A tall column of smoke drifted away aft of the stack. Charley found himself in a mood commensurate with Chapin's silence, a sleepy kind of mood with his mind clothed in a mist of uncertainties; the ocean's impenetrable vastness made for a silent, threatening loneliness that no amount of human company could offset. Out beyond the grinding paddles, not a single sound broke the stillness for hundreds of miles. He shook himself and looked at the pallid youth beside him; he said, "You look kind of young for this kind of business."

"So do you."

"That's different," Charley said. "I'm forty years older than I look."

68

The youth gave him a strange glance and, like a dog bristling against a faint unfamiliar scent, lifted his guard, pushing Charley out of his presence. It irritated Charley; he gave Chapin a deliberate glance and when the youth put cool, almost indifferent eyes on him, Charley said, "I'm in McDowell's company."

"So am I."

"We ought to stick together," Charley said. "You and me, we're the only ones in the bunch not old enough to vote."

"I don't want to vote," Carl Chapin said, and swung abruptly from the rail toward the hatch that led down by ladder into the cabin in the hold. Charley watched him go, angered a little by the youth's rebuff, but presently forgot about it and rested his lazy attention on the gray-green infinity of the sea. Fine short wrinkles converged around his eyes and he thought he could see, just on the eastern horizon, the rise of a blue strip of land. It was hard to tell; it might have been clouds.

He felt weight behind him and turned to see a heavy figure standing with a cool smile—Bill Randolph. Sudden apprehension went through Charley's nerves. A chill ran down his back and Bill said, "All healed up, kid?"

"I reckon so," he said, remembering a recent beating he had suffered at Bill's hands.

"That's good," Bill said. "I didn't mean you no harm. You made me kind of mad and I was in a lousy mood that day."

"Sure."

Charley had worked under Bill at the Triple Ace for a long time. He had come to know the big bartender's tempers. Sometimes Bill became loquacious. Today he seemed in one of those turns of mind; he said, "You know, it's a funny thing."

"What is?"

"There was a woman back in Sonora. You recollect the barmaid?"

"Gail? I remember her." Charley kept a seal on his expression.

"Night before we left, she damn near clawed me to death. See that scab on my neck?" Bill thrust his head forward, turning it, peeling back his dirty shirt collar with a finger.

"I see it."

"She's a bitch," Bill said, and hooked a bootheel over the lower rail. "All women are bitches. Good for one night at a time. You know that, kid?"

"Maybe," Charley said.

"Ain't no maybe about it. Ain't nothing so treacherous as a Goddamned woman." Bill turned and walked away. Five paces distant he paused and turned, and seemed about to speak. But he held his tongue. Charley looked curiously at him and Bill turned twice around, then said, "No hard feelings, hey, kid?"

Charley just looked at him. Bill said, "I mean it. I ain't got nothing against you. The bitch had me in a lousy mood and I took it out on you."

"All right," Charley said. "Forget it."

"You're a good kid," Bill said, and went.

Charley wondered what had prompted him. It didn't make much difference. Gail was a long way behind him, no more than a memory of brief friendship and brief pleasure. Perhaps Bill was right. The sea was all chopped up in little pieces and had a flinty glitter. The smell of it was part of everything. He stood with somber gravity, touched the small handful of coins in his pocket and knew that privation had at least taught him the unimportance of most of what he did not have. He wondered why he had come here and why the sea was.

He turned and went around to the starboard side and faced the west, the ocean without limits, and put his back to that when he knocked on Helen Zimmerman's door.

The first thing she said was, "I wanted to thank you."

"Never mind. How do you feel?"

"I feel fine," she said. "Come in, Charley."

She let him in and, he noticed, left the door open when she came around and sat on the edge of the bunk. Charley said, "Now that we've known each other two days, we ought to be old friends."

"What do you mean?"

He went to the door and put his hand on it as if about to close it; he looked across the deck at the gentle lift and drop of the sea, and he left the door as it was, turning around toward her.

She wore a dove-gray dress with a high collar and her slim, smooth hands were folded in her lap, oddly delicate against the heaviness of her body. Her face still showed high color, the mark of last night's adventure. Her eyes were round and smiled a little. The throb of engines kept the place vibrating. He sat down on the bunk with a space between them and looked sideways at her. He remembered a place he had seen once in the Sierra Nevadas where the trail passed through a rich meadow of deep tangled grass, and in the shallows of a creek clear water chuckled. He said, "Don't you get scared?"

"I was scared last night."

"I don't mean that."

"Then what?"

"You're the only woman on this boat. A hundred-odd men and damned few of them honest."

"You're honest, aren't you?"

He felt his nerves string tight. "No," he said. "Three days ago I stole a miner's poke."

Her glance drifted away. She had nothing to say, but he knew she was disappointed.

He studied his fingers, the grain of wood in the floorboards, the metal hasp of her trunk on the floor. "I gave the money back to his wife—his widow, I guess you'd say. He would have been robbed anyway. I just beat him to it."

"Who?"

"Another thief. The man who killed him. The one who got shot last night." He flicked a fast look, but her eyes were averted. She displayed a kind of brooding indifference. "Hey," he said. "I'm sorry."

"What for?"

He had no ready answer. "For saying anything. For rolling the miner. Maybe for giving the gold back. Hell, I don't know. I wish you didn't know about it—I wish it hadn't happened."

"You saw this man kill him?"

"Yes."

71

"But you didn't report it."

"No. I guess that wasn't right, was it?"

"I guess not," she said. Then he saw her eyes lift, full of something he could not identify, perhaps interest and perhaps fear, or something else altogether. He said, "I made a bad guess. Why is it you can be good all your life, and then do one bad thing, and be marked bad from then on?"

"You're only bad if you think you are." She was watching him earnestly but he didn't believe her. "You're not bad, Charley. Not after what you did last night."

"That was selfish."

"Was it?"

"Sure. I did it for myself. I like you."

"It's still not selfish. You could have stayed below where it was safe."

"They were all sick down there. It smelled like hell."

Her smile was gentle and it made him loosen up. He leaned back on his elbows and crossed his legs and threw his head back, staring at the ceiling. "Maybe I ought to say something about Parker to one of the officers." When she did not encourage him, he said, "Would you like me to do that?"

"Don't do anything on my account." She added, "Don't do anything until you know it's right."

"Well, then," he said, "what's right?"

"You've got to know that for yourself."

She wasn't much help. A breath of cool sea air came in through the open door; someone strolled by outside. He said, "I can't get your brother figured out."

"Why?"

"Last night when he caught me here, he picked a fight with me. I hit him a good one, and he quit cold. I figured him for a coward then. But later on, he came out there and hauled both of us inside out of the weather. That took guts."

"Maybe one thing was more important than the other," she said. "I was there, and if you'd hurt me, I would have said so. He knew that, and that's why he didn't keep fighting with you."

"I guess so." Charley thought about it. He found things rubbing off on him from all kinds of people. He let himself lie flat, legs dangling over the side of the bunk. His hands were laced under the back of his head and he felt the satisfying tough hardness of his stomach muscles stretching. Seeing the girl's turned face from the back and side, he watched her with grave care in silence until she said, "I don't ordinarily let men in my room."

"Smart," he said. "Maybe you shouldn't have let me in. I usually don't treat women as well as I've treated you."

She looked surprised. "Oh, now, you're not as tough as all that. I'm not afraid."

A sarcastic rejoinder crossed his mind and he thought it might be amusing to voice it, but he kept it to himself and was, thereafter, puzzled by his own reticence and sudden gentility before this girl.

"You're young, but you've known a few women," she said.

"None like you."

She made him feel that she regarded it as more than just a silly boyish compliment. Uneasy, he got to his feet and stood holding the edge of the door high in one hand. Half-leaning on his arm that way, he said, "I guess you and your brother won't be going on with us?"

"No. We'll stay in San Pedro."

A distinct regret crossed his feelings. "I guess that's better. It'll be a rough trip overland. Maybe I'll see you again when this is all over. Damn—we'll be in San Pedro tomorrow. Where will you be in a year's time?"

"I don't know."

"Well," he said, "you meet somebody and then you go away. Is that all there is to it?"

"If it is, isn't it good enough?" she asked. "We've had this much. We've met, we've learned a little about each other."

He felt disappointed and low. "It's a long way to Mexico."

"I'd like to see it sometime. They say it's very beautiful."

"I never thought of it that way," Charley said. "What's the name of the school you'll be at back East?"

"Here," she said. "I'll write it down for you."

When she handed him the slip of paper he looked at it as if it were clear to him, folded it carefully and put it in his pocket. "Will you write to me?" she said.

"Maybe. Maybe I will." He wandered toward the door. "We don't dock until tomorrow. I'll come back," he said, knowing he wouldn't. She directed a long, gentle look toward him. "So long," he said, and pulled the door closed.

Charley was alone on deck. Questions of destiny occupied his mind, overlaid by memories and apprehensions. The loneliness of the vast sea came close enough to touch him threateningly.

CHAPTER 10

For all his seeming indolence, Sus Ainsa was seldom far out of touch with news of importance. In the San Pedro hotel which headquartered them, and which would be the officers' last indoor quarters for some time to come, he came into Crabb's view at the suite doorway and knocked on the open door politely.

Crabb looked up and waved him forward, all the while considering his handsome, loose-jointed brother-in-law. He was perceptive enough to say, "You've found something out."

"Yes," Sus said. "There are some interesting dispatches from Ures and Hermosillo."

"Go on," Crabb said.

"There is also a very pretty young lady in the suite below," Sus said with a grin, and Crabb resigned himself to waiting the younger man out. Sus was always a man to lead up to things in his own good time. Now, in aggravating detail, he gave a description of the *señorita* who resided downstairs, and told of her circumstances. Beneath such trivialities Sus concealed a loyal heart and a considerable store of hardy courage. As a dandy, he left one suspicious; as a warrior, he made one impatient; as a lover, Crabb suspected Sus had added a good deal to his own legend that was not deserved. Nonetheless Crabb found himself comfortable in the young man's pleasant company, and was apt to confide in him things that he might not reveal to his own officers.

In time Sus let the subject of the downstairs lady drop, and said, "The news from Ures is that Pesquiera's man Aguilar is now seated in the governor's chair. For all practical purposes the revolt is successfully complete. The dispatch from Hermosillo states that Manuel Gandara has retreated to Mexico City, where he is bound to get no help at all. Jesús Gandara is up in the Sierra Madres with the Indians. His guerrillas have been destroyed by Pesquiera and Gabilondo. If the reports are not more exaggerated than usual, I think we must assume Pesquiera's coup is realized completely. He has no significant opposition any more."

"I see," Crabb said, and was reluctant to show his alarm. He stroked his brown beard and looked round the room with habitual vagueness in his eyes; he always gave the appearance of a man who had constant trouble keeping his mind on the subject at hand. This impression was only partly true. At the moment he was considering, with his quick politically trained mind, the varied and far-reaching implications of the news Sus had delivered. It was true he had anticipated Pesquiera's victory, but what he had not expected was that it would occur so quickly. There was danger in this, the matter of time.

Finally he returned his attention to Sus. The lean, graceful figure was clothed in the black finery of a *don*. "I think we'll wait until tomorrow night," Crabb said. "Then, when we're camped in the field, it will be time enough to advise the officers of this piece of news."

"Some of them may already know of it."

"Perhaps. But it will do no harm to wait until we are away from here. Once we're on the march, I'll have more confidence in my ability to control their feelings. There are too many distractions and temptations in a town like this one. I want no one backing out at this stage."

"As you wish," Sus said, and grinned. "I am to take it, then, that I am free for the evening?"

75

"Go on," Crabb said gruffly, waggling a hand. "Pay your respects to the young lady."

"My thanks for your kind understanding," Sus said, with the flash of a smile. He turned and went out, spurs dragging the floor.

When the door closed, Crabb clasped his hands behind him and paced the floor, brooding downward. Events were not as bright as he would have them. Presently he sat down at the writing desk and composed a letter to his wife in San Francisco. "*My dear Filomena*," he began, and stroked his nose with the feather of the pen. Dipping it into the inkwell, he wrote in his precise small hand an account of the voyage just past, a report of the storm at sea, and a number of paragraphs of hopeful anticipation in which he assured her of his coming victory and of all that it would mean to the fortunes of her family. He mentioned Sus's good health and conveyed his regards; out of habit he signed the letter, "*Y'r ob't svt, Henry.*" For a moment he sat pen in hand while an image came to him of the sweet composed smile that would curve her lips when the servant dropped the letter on her desk. She would walk across the parlor, a trim small figure of dark hair and eyes and a wistful smile that he had always liked. She would seat herself properly near the window and open the letter without hurry, and read with steady interest. . . . So Pesquiera had won already. It was a hard piece of news. But he could not turn back. He had too many commitments. He had made a contract with the men under him; he had an obligation, to them, to his family, to himself.

He sealed the letter and went downstairs to post it. In the lobby were a few knots of men, his various officers, and he stopped on his way back to the stair to have a word with Dr. Oxley. "That man who was shot," Crabb said, "what about him?"

"A severe wound," Oxley said. "He'll have to travel by wagon if he comes at all."

"We'll keep him," Crabb said. "I have made a contract with that man to deliver him to a homesite. Besides, we may have need of every pair of arms and every rifle."

"He's not much of a specimen. I think he's a jailbird."

"Have a bed made for him in one of the wagons," Crabb said, and turned away. He heard Oxley's "Very well," nodded to the others and climbed the steps. As he neared the top he found himself cursing his own shortness of breath. Years were telling in the dwindling vitality of his energies; he was, in fact, only thirty-five, but youth seemed a long way behind. He climbed the second flight and paused for breath, and went down the corridor to his room. Inside he poured a precisely measured ounce of whisky, downed it straight, and went to the window to look outward with brooding eyes. He was a man of varied moods and this evening a severe melancholia began to depress him. He wished Sus had stayed with him tonight; a few hours of the younger man's idle banter and insolent grin might have changed the sour taste on his tongue. When he looked forward into the coming weeks his feeling was bleak; he lay down on the bed, fully clothed, and took another drink while he began to pour himself earnestly back in time to a far and different past.

His thirty-five years had brought him a long way from Nashville. Now, through the open slit at the base of the window, he could hear the coarse cries of sailors on the waterfront, the rattle of wagons traveling the streets, the loud talk of a drunk. He got up to fill his glass, and found on the table a copy of Zimmerman's latest dispatch to the New York *Times*. He read it with a strange concentration.

"*It is reported that a plan exists to divide California, annex the Gadsden Purchase, and create a new Slave State. The idea is simply absurd.*"

Crabb smiled briefly. Not so long ago, the plan had not been so absurd. But like all careful politicians he had canvassed his friends in Sacramento. He remembered one colleague's words exactly: "If you want to make a new Slave State, Henry, don't try to make it out of existing territories. You haven't got the support." He allowed himself to relax with one shoulder against the window frame, looking upon the street. Above a distant building flapped a banner of the Know-Nothing party. For a time it had been Crabb's party. He had never particularly believed in the tenets of that organization—hatred in blanket form of all immigrants, notably the Irish, the German, the Catholics. It was difficult to maintain such an attitude in view of his wife's allegiance to the Church; it was even more difficult because the Know-Nothing platform straddled the slavery issue. But in California the power of the party had been strong and in it he had seen a chance to achieve a Senate seat in Washington. Unfortunately, in California senators were elected from the state congress—and he had a good many enemies there. His bid had been defeated. It had cut him loose, set him adrift. He regretted none of it, but from his presently detached position he was free to recognize the good fortune that had made his wife purposefully ignorant of politics. She had never shown any interest in his allegiances; her mind, shrewd in its way, recognized that he had merely seized an expedient means. She had never reproached him. Because of that, he felt both relief and a portion of guilt. He was happy to have it all behind him.

His glass was empty. He put it away and lay down. His eye tracked the course of a jagged crack in the ceiling. Tomorrow the journey would begin. He felt troubled by the news from Mexico; he knew Pesquiera, and thus he knew that Pesquiera was as much a political man as he himself was. His eyelids drew slowly together; he yawned.

*   *   *

A listless breath of air held a weary carpet of yellow dust hovering just above the ground. The early morning was cool. Men stood around shuffling their feet. Behind them a mile distant was the silhouette of the town, the wharves, the boats; and the green swell of the ocean. Above the meadow grew gnarled cypresses. Charley stood alone in the midst of the disorganized crowd of men, drawn off in small knots of quiet conversation. He considered a group of little white cloud balls that rolled softly across the sky, and remembered standing on the gangplank watching the buggy go away at a rapid clip with Zimmerman and the deep-eyed girl, neither of them looking back. People came into your life and went out of it.

Down at the foot of the meadow, Crabb and McDowell and

the other officers were holding a heads-together conference, the low-east sun shooting their shadows long and thin along the earth, and eighty or ninety men waited around in the cool dusty morning. Charley turned and drifted away from the murmuring crowd, going up into the hillside of flat-topped cypress ghosts, wind-blown into eerie shapes, and found presently that the forest was a cathedral, drilled through by dark, long-sounding corridors. Here he stood with his head thrown back, trembling a little against the dry cold. Underfoot the ground was a strange mixture of ocean-white sand and brush growth. He noticed the weight of the revolver, the dig of the rifle across his shoulder, the heaviness of the carpetbag and the hang of the coat; there was the jingle of coins in his pocket when his fingers touched them. From his belt hung the pouch full of round leaden bullets and a bag of black gunpowder with a little tin of percussion caps. He put down the carpetbag and took a tentative aim across the rifle's sights at a red cardinal that squatted at the base of a tree not far away. The cardinal blinked at him, pecked at the ground once or twice and, when Charley's foot moved, flapped away. Charley balanced the long-barreled rifle across his hand and wished it weighed less.

He put it over his shoulder and picked up the carpetbag, and pulled the hat low over his eyes as he had seen Norval Douglas do it. The hat was an unfamiliar tightness about his scalp, but Douglas had told him it would be needed on the desert. It was a wagon-hat, flat of crown and wide of brim, dun-colored like the dust that hovered below the woods.

When he looked back through the trees, down the way he had come, he could see far at the foot of the meadow the conference breaking up, the officers walking forward and General Crabb going toward a mound of earth. Regretfully, Charley turned with his equipment and went back into the open to join his company.

Men milled and gossiped. He saw Chuck Parker sitting in a camp chair, his injured leg bandaged, and Samuel Kimmel, who had shot him, watching over him like a hovering nurse. Parker was ignoring Kimmel; he was deep in heated conversation with Bill Randolph. Charley mingled into the crowd.

He saw David McDowell, who was the captain of his company, come up across the dry grass and signal to Norval Douglas and Will Allen. The two went away from the crowd and for a while there was a quiet conversation among these three men. Will Allen came from Coyote Flat, and was the company's lieutenant, a slight but muscular man with a drooping brown mustache that gave his whole expression a dour cast. Captain McDowell had a vivid red beard that chopped up and down when he talked. Norval Douglas did a good deal of listening, very little talking. Charley wondered what they were discussing.

A hand gripped his shoulder from behind, startling him. He frowned because he never liked to be touched. What he saw when he turned was Bill Randolph's sweat-caked stubbled face, and it made him go still inside and guard his expression with a tough screen. The big bartender grinned an unclean sort of grin, as if they were old friends among strangers, and said, "What you suppose they're jawing about, Charley?"

"How would I know?"

"I thought you were pretty friendly with Norval Douglas."

"What if I am? He doesn't tell me everything."

"Just thought I'd ask," Bill said mildly. He seemed in an amiable mood; he let Charley's hard tones ride off him. Chuck Parker's voice lifted to a bellow, hailing him, and he drifted off. Idlers milled around. Charley had a glimpse of Jim Woods and of Carl Chapin, the indrawn youth he had met at the ship's rail. Chapin was standing by himself, his Adam's apple like a second chin, looking waspish and bad-tempered. Charley felt the uneasiness of waiting begin to build. Men moved around aimlessly, restlessly, striking up conversations and letting them drop incomplete, looking half-apprehensively at Captain McDowell and his little council, and presently almost in a mass shifting their attention to the solitary jut-bearded figure of General Crabb, who had climbed the little mound of earth and now stood with his hands behind him and his head down. Someone spoke nearby and Charley let himself eavesdrop out of idleness. "I reckon Crabb wants to take over Sonora and get himself appointed the first senator from Sonora."

"You're crazy," was the reply. "You think ninety men can take over the whole state of Sonora?"

"We've got more coming. Talk is, General Cosby's in San Francisco organizing a party of a thousand men. They're supposed to sail down the Mex coast to Port Lobos and cut across Sonora to meet us at Altar. That way we'll have the Mexicans between two jaws—we'll make hash out of them."

"Not with no hundred men, we won't. I don't believe that, not a bit."

"Just the same, I reckon it's true."

"Well, it don't make no never-mind to me anyway. Long as I get what I been promised. You ever been down in Mexico?"

"No."

"I was there in 'Fifty-two. Gold and silver lying around to be picked up. Never seen nothing like it."

"How come you didn't stay?"

"I was lucky I got out with my skin. Prospected a couple months in the Madres, and got run out by a bunch of Mexes. They don't cotton much to gringos down there."

"Then how come you're going back now?"

"I expect there's enough of us to be safe. Besides, these repeater pistols ought to scare them off."

The two men moved away beyond earshot, and Charley spent a time considering what he had heard. None of it was particularly new, but it crystallized something in his mind and made him begin to wonder actively just what he was doing here. Somehow he had drifted into this thing and let it carry him along with it, never quite knowing very much about it at all. Everything was vague, tenuous—strange promises of land and mineral deposits; he knew little of farming and nothing of mining. What had it to offer him? Was there a past or a future? There was no past he could return to; there was nothing certain about the future. Maybe death on the Devil's Road. He had heard of that, well enough: a desert of sand and cactus, lined with the white bones of animals and men.

Around him the crowd milled like an ant colony, staying close to one another in a packed bunch as if to protect itself against something evil. Questions, unvoiced, traveled across the short spaces between men and made them all wary. *Spooked*, Charley thought, and looked at Norval Douglas, out on the meadow a little way distant with the captain and lieutenant. Douglas was the one firm rock amid all this confusion—a man who never displayed uncertainty. What surprised Charley when he thought about it was how little, after all, he knew about Douglas. But Douglas owned a calm of features and a bleak but positive self-assurance in his yellow eyes, and these things seemed like buoys in a tossing sea that was without a place to anchor.

The council broke up and Douglas came toward the crowd with Will Allen, while Captain McDowell set off across the grass toward the earth-hump where General Crabb stood in his thoughtful pose. Something about that picture of Crabb in the near distance, alone on a tiny hilltop, reminded Charley of an illustration of George Washington he had seen somewhere. Crabb wore no hat and the breeze lifted his hair, moving it lightly. His eyes were dark and brooding. Captain McDowell approached him, red beard chopping when he talked, and Crabb listened with courteous interest, afterward making a brief answer; thereupon McDowell made a smart about-face and came back toward the company.

McDowell planted his feet and called the company to attention. There being no real military discipline in the group, the effect of the command was mainly to muffle conversations and turn curious eyes forward. McDowell stroked his red beard and eyed the company skeptically—it was rumored he was a West Point man—and spoke in a voice calculated to draw attention: "Let's have a little quiet, gentlemen."

When the foot-shuffling and coughing and story-concluding was done, McDowell turned his back to the company and stood facing Crabb, hands behind his back and feet spread. Down the line, Captains Holliday and McKinney likewise silenced their companies and swung away to stand at ease watching the general. Charley observed the hip-slanted posture of Captain Bob Holliday of Company B, and found himself wondering whether perhaps Holliday wasn't easier to get along with than McDowell, who stood with a certain spine-stiffness that indicated arrogance.

These were the flats of El Monte, and supplies stood stacked beyond Crabb's outline. The horse remuda was down there staked out, and Crabb's five Conestoga wagons waited, hitched each to sixteen mules. The general drew himself up and faced the command; and spoke in a bell-clear voice:

"Gentlemen, this is truly an auspicious occasion. We stand today on the threshold of a great experiment. The continued prosperity of America may well depend on your strength, your steadfastness, your courage."

Someone within Charley's hearing muttered petulantly, "Get done with the politics, General, and let's get to riding."

Crabb launched into his speech, a thunder of energy and rhetoric punctuated by wide sweeping gestures and occasional beard-tugging. It was the same kind of talk Charley had heard before—a call to loyalty and duty, a warning that laxity could breed danger, a promise of rich lands and lodes for the colonists. Behind Charley, at intervals, the petulant kibitzer would mutter a comment. "What the hell is he talkin' about?"

"Shut up, Shorty," said another voice. "He's making sense."

"Yeah? Sounds like chicken-clucking to me, that's what I think. Chicken-clucking."

"Shut up, Shorty."

Crabb waved his arms, promising riches beyond a man's imagining. Manifest destiny, Crabb talked of—the destiny of an entire continent to become one nation. "Are we to allow our land to stagnate in a slack eddy of time while just to the south of us a vast and wealthy ground lies fallow? Gentlemen, no!" And more, and more. Charley planted his feet and folded his arms and stood through it without being touched by it; it was merely one of those countless things he put back in his mind for storage, and now and then would draw out to regard briefly before returning it to its pigeonhole. "In Mexico today," Crabb said, "there is a man of peace—a man of democracy—a man who speaks no treachery against the United States. That man is our friend. His name is Ignacio Pesquiera."

"And," the muttering Shorty grumbled, "he happens to be your wife's cousin. Don't try foolin' us, Crabb."

The muttered comment barely reached Charley. Crabb had paused momentarily; now he drew up his chest and stood with his blocky figure very solid and very self-assured; he tugged his brown beard with his fingers and said, "No one is bound to us. No one need stay. You are free to go home if you wish. The road on which we embark today is a road of hardship and danger. I will blame no man who wishes to leave us. But if you must, quit us today; for the road back will become more difficult as we march farther from this port. Gentlemen?"

"Long as I get paid," Shorty muttered, "I stick."

A murmur of apprehensive talk ran around the gathering; but no one moved, and in a moment Crabb said, "Very well. Captains, organize your companies. Mount your men. Be prepared to march in one hour. That's all—and the best of luck to every man."

Crabb stepped off the hump of land and walked slowly away across the yellow grass. A cloud was crossing the sun. Its sharp-rimmed shadow swept across the meadow, overtaking Crabb and covering him. His choppy-striding figure passed the piled supplies and disappeared behind a wagon. Charley shifted the weight of the rifle on his shoulder and saw Captain McDowell open his mouth to utter a command.

CHAPTER 11

The man who came walking unhurriedly up the sharp tilt of the sidewalk was small and trim, and dressed in a conservative gray business suit which he had selected with some care. It was a quiet street; below nearer the harbor teemed the San Francisco traffic. The bantam pedestrian was plainly of Mexican heritage —his dark skin, angled eyes, and straight glistening black hair revealed that much. He skipped the point of a cane lightly along the walk. His glance was speculative. The wind had driven fog off the bay and now the morning sun rippled off its surface beyond the docks; from this hillside he could see across the tops of the city buildings to the islands and the vague blue rim of land across the bay. He turned up a weatherbeaten stair that took him onto a wooden porch, and lifted the brass knocker.

An Oriental opened the door and gave him a polite look. He said, "This is General Cosby's residence?"

"Yes."

"I wish to see him. My name is Cassio."

He stepped inside. The houseboy said, "One moment please," and went back through the house. Cassio removed his hat and looked idly around the dim hall until the houseboy came back, took his hat and cane, and led him into a furnished study. Behind him he heard the door close quietly.

The desk was near the bay window. The man behind the desk was round-cheeked and wore a pince-nez. A paunch was beginning to swell at his midriff. He said gruffly, "Señor Cassio?"

"Yes. I have come recently from Hermosillo."

"I see," Cosby said. Cassio felt dry amusement at the care with which Cosby concealed his curiosity. Cassio said, "Three days ago I passed through San Pedro. General Crabb's party had left there a week before, about one hundred men strong. He was outfitted with five prairie schooners. They carried food for sixty days. By now I would suspect they have passed Warner's Ranch."

Cosby was frowning. "Why do you bring this news to me?"

"I thought you might find it interesting," Cassio murmured, and smiled gently.

"All right," Cosby said. "What do you want?"

Cassio could see that the general was not a man to whom amenities meant much. It would be best, he decided, to come immediately to the point. He said, "I have it on good authority that you have been commissioned to raise an army of a thousand men and take them by sea to reinforce Crabb in Mexico."

"Is that so?" Cosby said.

"I was not aware it was a secret."

"Go on," Cosby said.

Cassio had to smile. He said, "Let us say that I represent a group of financial men in Sonora. These men know of your—or rather, of Señor Crabb's agreement with Ignacio Pesquiera. But they are troubled. They recall quite well that when *Norteamericanos* were allowed to settle colonies in Texas, the results were not good for Mexico."

"I see," Cosby said. His voice was a scrape. "You've come up here to warn me—to threaten us, is that it? I can advise you right now it won't work. Bigger men than you have tried to frighten me."

Cassio waved a hand deprecatingly. "Nothing of the kind, I assure you. No one wishes to endanger you."

"In that case, you have conveyed the feelings of your friends. I acknowledge your concern. Now, if you don't mind, I have things—"

"One moment," the Mexican said smoothly. "Perhaps you do not appreciate the extent to which my associates are troubled. You see, for us it would not be a good thing at all if anything were to happen to the present regime in Sonora."

"Gandara's or Pesquiera's?"

Cassio chuckled. "Señor Gandara is quite finished, I assure you. My associates are quite satisfied with things as they are."

Cosby's eyes narrowed. "You can assure them, señor, that General Crabb and I wish no harm to Pesquiera."

"Can I?" Cassio murmured, and immediately smiled amiably. "No matter. My point is this: it might cause much apprehension among our people if a large force of armed men were to arrive on our shores under your command. So agitated, the people would perhaps begin to question the good intent of our present government. Now, Sonora has just suffered a lengthy and tiring revolution. No one wishes to see the tables turn at this late hour. You see my point?"

"Maybe," Cosby said. "What do you expect me to do about it?"

"Ah," Cassio breathed. "Exactly. Many of us would be quite happy if your thousand-man force failed to materialize."

Cosby merely looked at him expressionlessly. Cassio allowed

86

himself to smile. "Crabb himself is within the limits of his agreement with Pesquiera. He advances with a small party—less than a hundred men. His ostensible purpose is to seek out a site for a future colony. Very well, let him; the damage is now done. But if a large armed force were to come around by sea and meet him— that, then, would be beyond the limits of his agreement. It would be, I can promise you, tantamount to an act of war. Do I make myself understood, señor?" There was, abruptly, a bite in Cassio's smooth tone.

"I thought," Cosby rumbled imperturbably, "that you didn't intend to threaten me. What do you call this?"

"Advice," Cassio replied. His smile returned. "My friends in Hermosillo are quite wealthy. I have been empowered to make a rather substantial offer on their behalf—in the nature of a payment for insurance, one might say."

This was the moment he had prepared for; he stood now waiting tautly, his smile hovering, watching Cosby and trying to make out Cosby's reaction.

If Cosby was startled, he made no show of it. One eyebrow cocked up, and he removed his pince-nez to blow dust from the lenses. When he put them on his nose again, he said, "I see. What makes you suspect I might be inclined to accept that kind of an offer?"

"The size of the offer," Cassio answered promptly, softly.

"Which is?"

"Fifty thousand dollars," Cassio said mildly, and added, "In gold."

Cosby steepled his fingers. His lips pursed. Cassio found himself disliking the man intensely. A wagon clattered by on the cobblestones outside, wooden brakes scraping against the downhill slope. Presently Cosby looked up and said one word.

"Done."

Shortly thereafter, with a pleasant smile illuminating his face, Cassio left the house and strolled down toward Market Street. He was comfortable with the knowledge that General Cosby was no longer a threat to the peace.

*   *   *

Late afternoon. Sun in his face, turning it crimson, Captain David McDowell stood in the triangular opening of the tent, holding its flap back and waiting for the others to come up. McDowell's red beard was turned to livid flame by the low sun. He saw Sus Ainsa, dressed in black and looking very lean and supple, cruising the company street. Shortly a man came along, Freeman McKinney, captain of C Company, a tall man with a bald head that rose to a kind of point. McKinney, never a talkative soul, nodded briefly to McDowell and stooped to go into the tent. McDowell stayed where he was and saw the bottom rim of the sun flatten against the horizon. A long lance of bright pastel vermilion shot forward from the setting orb.

Presently Norval Douglas came along, dressed in mountain buckskins. McDowell took note of the yellow glitter of Douglas's eyes; it had never failed to unnerve him. Douglas also leaned and entered the tent, and when the sun had dropped another degree and the sheet of pastel hues had spread across the entire western quarter of the sky, with reds and yellows the color of brilliant limestone cliffs, then Bob Holliday came swinging down the path with long-legged, easy strides. Holliday was handsome and clean-shaven; he had an amiable smile and presented an elongated, raw-boned figure in the strange rose light of the dying day.

Holliday was in command of B Company, and McDowell's lips pinched together tautly when Holliday grinned lazily, said, "Evenin', Dave," and curled inside the tent like a long uncoiling snake. McDowell bit his lip and stooped to go inside, letting the flap fall behind him so that it became suddenly dark within the tent, and almost simultaneously, Freeman McKinney said, "Hey, somebody got a candle?" and Norval Douglas lighted the wick of a whale-oil lantern. That little incident impressed on McDowell the different ways of thinking of Douglas and McKinney.

"Pin the flap back, Dave," Douglas said in his quiet drawl. "Let's have some light in here."

McDowell turned around and folded the tent-flap back. On the rim of the earth, the sun was an overturned bowl angry in hue. Long shadows zigzagged along the ground. McDowell sat down Indian fashion, cross-legged, in the triangle of the opening, and swept his companions' faces.

"What's the trouble, Dave?" Freeman McKinney said.

"I thought we ought to have a little talk between us," McDowell said, "before we get too far out in the desert."

"What about?"

"The general," McDowell said, referring to Crabb.

There was a brief interval of silence, with red sundown light painting their faces before him, and Bob Holliday said in his casual tone, "What's wrong with the general?"

"I'm worried," McDowell answered. "About him and about us."

"Why?"

"For one thing, I don't like the way he waited until we were twenty miles out in the desert before he told us what he'd found out from Mexico. He may not have said so, but it seems clear to me that the turn of things down there throws a whole new light on what we're doing."

"What you mean is," Holliday suggested, "you don't trust Pesquiera."

"No," McDowell agreed. "I don't. He doesn't need us any more. His troops don't have anybody to fight—they're free to fight off the Apaches themselves. What does he need us for?"

"I'm sure," said Freeman McKinney, "that the general's thought about that. He knows what he's doing."

"Does he?" McDowell said quickly. "He's a politician, not a soldier."

"What of it?" Holliday said.

"When the time comes for military decisions," McDowell said, "do we leave them up to Crabb?"

"You always were a worrier," Holliday observed, and stretched his lanky legs along the tent's grass floor. He was leaning back, propped up on his elbows, and his eyes were sleepy.

"Another thing," McDowell added. "We've got to decide whether we're going to act like a bunch of colonists or a regiment of soldiers. You can't have it both ways. But the general keeps seesawing—from one minute to the next I can't tell if he aims to immigrate or invade. I think we ought to take it up to him. Frankly, I want a clear answer before we go any farther."

Holliday's half-lidded eyes rose. "The trouble with you West Point boys is you never know what to do until somebody gives you an order. Hell, Dave, why not go over to his tent and ask him?"

McDowell ignored the man's amiable insult; he answered, "Because we haven't agreed among ourselves yet."

"What's there to agree on?"

McDowell looked around. The dying sun cast softer shadows. In the corner, Norval Douglas sat silent, a man to whom stillness was important. McKinney's bald head gleamed and he frowned at his hands. Holliday looked mild and unconcerned. "Are we game for anything at all?" McDowell asked.

McKinney's frown turned toward him. "What's that supposed to mean?"

"I mean," McDowell said in precisely pronounced words, "are we all willing to stand behind the general no matter what happens?"

"I still don't follow you," McKinney said.

"Crabb's playing politics," McDowell said. "He's trying to play Pesquiera off against Gandara. But it won't work, because Gandara doesn't have a thimbleful of supporters left. Crabb was hoping that they'd weaken each other enough so that we could step in against nothing more than token opposition. But it didn't work out that way. Damn it, when we started this thing I knew what was up. I expected all along that we'd find ourselves trying to boost Henry Crabb into the Governor's Palace at Ures, or maybe the U. S. Senate from Sonora. It was a risky thing then, but it's a fool's play now. Pesquiera isn't half so weak as we thought he'd be. But Crabb goes right on ahead as if nothing had happened. I don't think he's fooling anybody— and I want to know if all of you are willing to take the risks."

"Are you?" McKinney countered.

Holliday's drawl broke in between them. "If you gents haven't got the guts for it, what are you doing here in the first place?"

"I just want to know how far out I'm going to have to stick

my neck—and how many men I can count on to stand with me," McDowell said. "Does that make me a coward?"

It was Norval Douglas who answered. "You're the only one who can answer that, Dave. But it seems to me that if you signed up to follow Crabb, then you're duty-bound to follow him wherever he heads."

"Is that the way you feel about it, Norval?"

"It is. I took a job. I intend to fulfill my end of the contract."

McDowell turned his troubled gaze out from the tent, across the brush-studded desert toward the westward peaks across which they had come. Ahead, southeast, lay the salt flats, the sand dunes that led finally to the banks of the Rio Colorado. The sun was down and indigo shadows spread thick along the ground. He thought of these men, his fellow officers. McKinney was an ex-member of the California legislature, one of Crabb's fellow politicians. He would probably follow Crabb's lead—or would he? Bob Holliday was a man of varied backgrounds; he had been a scout with Cooke's Mormon Battalion and he had fought with Frémont in California, but essentially he did not own the military mind. Of the other officers, not gathered here, he thought he might be able to count on Will Allen, his lieutenant and friend, and perhaps on Quarles and Porter, who were Holliday's lieutenants. Of the others he was not so sure. John Henry, from Mariposa, was McKinney's lieutenant and also an ex-member of the state legislature, as was the surgeon, Dr. Oxley. Colonel W. H. McCoun, whom Crabb saw fit to call his Commissary General, was likewise a former legislator, and had at one time stood tall in the state house. He would no doubt follow Crabb to the shores of the Styx if he had to. Other officers—Tozer and Bob Wood and Nat Wood and Ted Johns—were present at Crabb's suffrage. McDowell thus felt in the minority. He said as much: "The general's got himself surrounded by friends. But I don't want to be the sacrifice of a fool's mission."

"What do you want to do about it?" countered Holliday.

"I wish I knew."

"Why don't you sleep on it?" McKinney said. That was McKinney's answer to a good many things.

"I've slept with it for weeks," McDowell told him. "I'm at the point where I don't like it. I think we ought to find out exactly what the general has in mind before we go any farther."

"As I said before," Holliday drawled, "why don't you ask him?"

McDowell made no reply. The trouble was, he was afraid of what Crabb's answer might be—and he did not wish to be the only man in the party in disagreement with the general. He did not want events to make him out a coward; it was that simple. If at this point he refused to follow Crabb further, it would be akin to mutiny. If, thereafter, Crabb proved successful, McDowell would be behind, a castaway; and if Crabb proved unsuccessful, McDowell would be a scapegoat. He feared both consequences. He pounded his fist into an open palm. "Isn't anybody else interested in what we're headed for?"

"Maybe you should have thought all that out before you came along, Dave," said McKinney. "The rest of us did."

McDowell rolled out of the tent opening and stood up. In the east, over the desert flats, the moon was coming up with a soft ring of dust around it. He felt the pressure of time. Along the tent streets fires glittered, red gleams like eyes winking at him. Soft laughter swept across the evening and somewhere down the row a harmonica made sad melodies. Norval Douglas came out of the tent and put his light eyes on him; Douglas said, "Whatever you decide to do, Dave, don't let public opinion push you around." Then he swung away, a buckskinned figure moving through the night with a cougar's grace. The moonlit plain glimmered silver. When Bob Holliday appeared at the front of the tent, he merely showed a bleak expression, saying nothing, disappearing toward his own tent. Finally McKinney came out, moonlight glancing off the dome of his head, and stood with a musing pucker to his lips while he packed his pipe. "Dave."

"What?"

"It's likely to be a rough road. I suggest you make up your mind."

"I see," McDowell said slowly. "You don't trust me."

McKinney, for a politician, was blunt enough. "That's right," he said without malice. "If we ride into trouble, I want to know that the man who commands the left flank isn't occupied with trying to balance his own skin against the company's. Maybe you ought to figure out where your loyalties lie before we hit the Mexican line. I think you ought to do that, Dave."

"Thanks," he said drily.

McKinney made no reply. He put a match to the bowl of his pipe and when it was going to his satisfaction, he walked away.

CHAPTER 12

At the gray break of dawn the column moved out. Past Warner's Ranch and Sackel's Well now, they pushed southeastward toward Jeager's Ferry at the Yuma Crossing. Horsemen rode in a column of twos; out ahead of the regiment rode a single buckskin-clad man: Norval Douglas, trail scout. In the midst of the column plodded five Studebaker wagons, each drawn by eight spans of mules, with the driver riding the off wheel animal. On these laden wagons rode bedrolls, clothes, horse feed, tools, kegs of gunpowder, surgeon's supplies, water barrels, spare wheels and axles, flour barrels and salt pork and food to provision a hundred men for two months less the fortnight they had already traveled, and planks—many stout planks lashed beneath the wagons. When Charley had asked the meaning of these planks he had learned that they were to be used as rails for the wagons when they reached the forty-mile stretch of the soft sand-dune country. January—and the desert was smoky with ninety-degree heat. It was unseasonable and dismal; not a cloud appeared anywhere on the topaz expanse of the sky. Catclaw, greasewood, prickly pear, jointed cholla, barrel cacti—these seemed the only vegetation studding the gentle undulations of the land. "The land that God forgot," muttered Jim Woods,

93

riding at Charley's stirrup. Dust, kicked up by the column of horses ahead, filled his nostrils and caked his skin and formed a salty grit against his eyelids and tongue. There was the muffled tramp of hoofs, the creak of saddle leather, now and then a soft jingle of bit chains, the scrape of big wagon wheels and the listless flap of canvas.

The earth, tan-gray and rocky, became steadily softer underfoot as they moved into the rising sun morning after morning. Dull heat smothered the plain from midmorning to sundown. Mica particles in the ground flashed painfully against the eye. Seldom was there any wind; now and then came a sluggish current of air to scorch dry skin. Powerful sunlight burned their hands and faces and shoulders. Once, some distance back, Charley caught sight of Bill Randolph and Chuck Parker. Parker rode the tailgate of a wagon; Randolph, alongside, rode with his shirt off, his massive brown torso gleaming with brown sweat.

On the nineteenth they hit the dunes.

Wagon wheels sank almost hub-deep in the soft sand. The column halted. From the head of the line came commands, relayed back man to man. Charley found himself detailed with a small group of men near the second wagon. He stepped down and handed the reins of his horse to old John Edmonson, who scraped the back of his hand across a sweating weathered brow and attempted a smile. Leaving his rifle in the saddle boot, Charley plodded forward through the sand while it sucked at his boots.

Lieutenant Will Allen came up, a trim little man who twisted the points of his brown droopy mustache and said, "All right. Untie those planks under the wagon bed."

He had to crawl under the wagon to undo some of the knots. There was not much space between the wagon's floor and the tops of the sand dunes; the wagon had sunk practically to its axles. He had to dig his way in. His fingers were clumsy with the knots. He heard Lieutenant Allen's impatient voice: "Hurry it up, can't you?"

"Yes, sir," he muttered, and presently the ropes came loose. The planks almost dropped on his upturned face. He scrambled out from under the wagon and pulled the planks out, seeing another youth—Carl Chapin—doing the other side of the wagon.

Chapin ignored him. Charley went in again, and again, and after four trips had a stack of planks lying behind the wagon—four planks, each almost eighteen feet long. Chapin had the same kind of stack on his side. Charley stood breathing heavily, awaiting a command, curiously regarding the pale thin youth with the underslung chin. Chapin seemed more surly than ever; he glared with open malice at the lieutenant, who was motioning to Bill Randolph and three or four other men. "You'll find shovels in the wagon," the lieutenant said. "Dig it out."

Bill lifted his hat and scratched his head. "That's a powerful lot of diggin', Lieutenant."

"Do what you're told," Allen said, and swung away to inspect the next wagon down the line. His horse's hoofs kicked up high splashes of loose white sand; it plodded away as though half swimming.

Charley went back to his horse and stood by the stirrup while Bill and his crew poked their shovels into the sand beneath the wagon. In ten minutes Bill was swearing in a steady monotone. With every shovel of sand that was taken away, half a shovelful sifted back into the hole. "Jesus," Bill said. "This will take a week."

Old John Edmonson, holding Charley's horse, smiled gently and murmured, "The devil's work is never done." His talk was not loud enough to reach Bill's ears, and Charley felt thankful for that. He said, "Have you got any idea how far the dunes go?"

"About forty miles, I understand," said Edmonson.

By midafternoon the wagons were shoveled almost clear. Lieutenant Allen came back up the line, ordering the lounging men back into their saddles. When he came by, he stopped and spoke to Charley: "You and these five men will lay rails for this wagon." It was all he said; he reined his horse around and went forward toward the point.

The sun slapped hard against the earth, against the men. A tired stream of insects, they wound slowly forward across the

95

sea swells and troughs of the white glittering dunes. With each ten feet the wagon traveled, a board had to be taken up behind it and carried around to the front, where a man had to avoid somehow the plodding hoofs of the mules and still get the plank laid butt against the previous plank, which would by then be disappearing under the wheel. Thus continuous rails were kept under the wheels; and the expert muleskinners did their best to keep the heavy Conestogas on the tracks. On the uphill slopes men had to dismount and put shoulders to the wagon tailboards; on the downhill slopes the muleskinners leaned forward braced against the ropes of the brake handles, and men rode behind with ropes dallied from saddlehorns to the wagon. Horses waded almost to the stirrups in the liquid sand. The westering sun stretched shadows and poured rivulets of sweat down the flesh of straining, red-eyed men.

Often a plank would tilt, slide, slip away; the wagon would sag; men would ride up, dab ropes over the wheel hub and haul the wheel up out of the dry quagmire until the plank could be righted. Once, resetting a plank in this way, Charley almost lost his hand under a wheel that came plunging away from a rope that slipped loose.

Night made its approach. In five hours the train had advanced less than half a mile. The mules were unhitched, fed and watered, and hobbled with the horse stock. Campfires blossomed in the evening and over the desert, indigo and violet twilight swept in a last retreating defense. Charley ate his meal and sank back on his blanket exhausted, his muscles trembling. Norval Douglas crouched cross-legged frowning into the fire, his eyes gleaming frostily. Jim Woods came up from the wagon and packed his tin utensils away, scrubbed clean with sand, and joined the small group around the fire. Around them the tent streets were quiet and lonely. The wheezing harmonica that they had become accustomed to was silent tonight. Charley stretched his shoulders. The air turned crisp and the fire's warmth made him immediately sleepy. A newcomer drifted up and stood a diffident six paces from the fire, looking forward inquiringly, and when Charley turned to look at him he recognized old

John Edmonson. When he had taken time to study Edmonson, Norval Douglas said, "Rest a while."

"Thanks," Edmonson said, and crouched down, turning his open palms toward the blaze. Downslope beyond the tents, guards walked slow circles around the picketed horses, now and then stopping close to one another to converse. A final ribbon of cobalt dusk faded away westward. John Edmonson stared into the fire. His cheeks were stubbled with gray and his face seemed even more deeply lined than Charley remembered it. Edmonson nodded courteously to Jim Woods and a moment later pulled out a briar pipe and packed it with care, leaning forward then to poke a twig into the fire. He put it to his pipe and puffed deeply until a red-gray spiral of smoke began to rise from the bowl, whereupon he tossed the twig on the fire and sat back, pulling contentedly on the smoke. Red-bearded Captain McDowell came up looking troubled and dipped his head to them all, and made a space for himself, saying, "This will be the last fire we'll be able to build for some time. There's no fuel on the dunes. We ought to roll in soon—we'll be on the move at sunrise. We'll be lucky to make a mile a day." He stared across the fire. "Norval, you'll ride out at midnight. I want you to find the shortest route across the dunes."

"Due east," Douglas said promptly. "Thirty-eight miles. After that, Yuma Crossing and the Sonora desert. We're starting a little late in the season, I'm afraid—the desert will be damned hot by the time we reach it."

"We'll do all right," McDowell said in a way that at first sounded confident; afterward Charley began to feel the man was trying to reassure himself. "Those of us who are strong enough, anyway," McDowell added. "And the others have no business coming." His glance drifted across the face of old Edmonson; there was no visible break in his expression. He stood up and said, "Good night, gentlemen," and went away into the night.

"Checking on the troops," Jim Woods observed. "McDowell takes things too damned seriously, I think."

"That's his job," Norval Douglas murmured. Charley sat up to let his belly bake against the fire. He looked at Edmonson, who sat drawing on his pipe, apparently at peace with himself and ignoring the comment that McDowell seemed to have directed at him; Edmonson appeared to be a good deal older than he should have been for this kind of an expedition. He said now, "I gather that our friend the captain believes that things must be done in a hurry."

"That's Crabb's belief," Woods said. "It rubs off on the officers."

"Many a mistake has been made because of haste," Edmonson said, squinting through his pipe smoke.

Douglas was leaning back with one elbow on the ground, looking off across the swells of the dunes. "I expect you'll find the world's work gets done by men in a hurry, Mr. Edmonson," he said.

"Perhaps," Edmonson said. He did not appear to agree.

Douglas said, "I recall that we were too slow on the march in Lower California, in 'Fifty-four. That was why we were defeated."

"You were with the William Walker party?"

"I was."

"You must be a filibuster at heart, then," Edmonson said.

Douglas poked a twig into the corner of his mouth and let it tilt there; it waggled when he talked. "Adventure is where you find it."

"What happened to that expedition?"

"We were licked," Douglas said. His tone indicated no particular regret. "We landed down there and Walker proclaimed it an independent republic—all of Baja and Sonora. But that's a bitter country and he hadn't brought enough food or water. You can't live off the land when the land supports nothing but twigs and spines and rocks. The Mexicans starved us out and we had to retreat overland to San Diego. It was a rough hike."

"Walker's done better since then," Jim Woods said.

"That he has," Edmonson agreed. "I understand he's got control of the Nicaraguan government."

Douglas's shoulder moved. "He won't last. The natives are against him."

"They'll be against us too, more'n likely," Woods said.

"We can handle it, if it comes to that."

"What makes you so sure?" Edmonson said.

"Just a feeling," Douglas told him. "I think we all need sleep. Let's turn in."

*   *   *

Planks broke or overturned. Wagon wheels slipped off and sank hub-deep in sand. In the depths of the dunes, each such occurrence meant the wagon must be unloaded, for there was no shoveling this loose liquid sand. The wheels had to be reset on the plank rails and the wagon reloaded. Days passed with a dreadful monotony. Toward the end of January the weather turned cool and cloudy, but there was no rain. Nighttime temperatures plunged down into the thirties; men shivered by night and sweated by day. McDowell's estimate had been correct; there were days when they did not make a full mile. By the tenth day of February, with the Colorado still twenty miles distant, water for the animals was reduced to one ration every forty-eight hours. Mules began to drag in their traces and had to be shot. The column moved day and night now; one shift of men would sleep, then catch up and relieve the other half of the party. The shifting, treacherous sandhills made of it a trek through hell. Food spoilage made scurvy a danger. On the seventeenth, they found that too many planks had splintered; they could not move all the wagons at the same time. With ten miles yet to go, the pace slowed again; each wagon in turn had to wait on its rails while the spare planks were carried to other wagons. Norval Douglas led a party ahead to the military post above Jeager's Ferry, but there was little food to be spared at that outpost. It was all Douglas and his detail could do to return with four water barrels filled at the river, two sacks of flour and a side of bacon. Men ate sourdough biscuits and gnawed on strips of leather-hard beef jerky. On the twenty-seventh of February they rolled out of the desert and turned upstream to Jeager's Ferry. At the Army post they recruited a few mules. Crabb sent a dispatch to San Francisco, and directed Charles Tozer and Robert Wood to ride with all possible speed to Tucson, where they were to recruit additional men to reinforce the column when it reached Mexico. George Alonzo Johnson's clumsy steamboat was moored above the ferry, which had a bloody history of its own; Captain Johnson grinned and waved a hand as the column marched upriver. The river was rising with the first of spring's melted snow from the mountains up the Colorado and Gila and Salt. Arizona lay ahead of them, sunlit and brassy.

So many mules had been shot and eaten during the clumsy crossing of the dunes that several horses had to be hitched into the teams, setting a squad of men afoot. Nonetheless, a construction mechanic at Fort Yuma who asked the men what they intended to feed their horses along the desert *Jornada* got the cheerful reply that they would ride them into the shops and feed them calico. There was a reckless spirit of abandon alive in the party, stirred up perhaps by the cool crossing of the river and the path they now traveled up the Gila River, easy going after what lay behind them. The word "filibuster" came out in the open and men laughed with it; those who made rational justification for the march were pushed away and the spirit of impending conquest fixed its grip on them, so that soon with few exceptions, and for the first time, the many individuals bonded together with a single purpose. Captain McDowell's face lost its look of troubled uncertainty and he joined himself to the other officers with positive enthusiasm; the anticipation of manifest victory was all about.

In a wagon bed rode Chuck Parker, his fever risen and broken, his leg healing slowly. One-eyed Sam Kimmel, who had shot him, walked alongside and periodically inquired after Parker's needs.

Several men came down with various ailments. It was to be expected. Sus Ainsa found himself put in charge of this group, and watched over it with good cheer.

Forty-five miles east of Yuma they made a halt to rest and organize for the desert crossing ahead. The party now numbered eighty-nine; a few men had left at Yuma and two or three recruits had joined the expedition. Here, in a shaded oasis of cottonwoods and grass, tents were pitched and horses and mules grazed while men cut their names in cottonwood bark and christened the spot Filibuster Camp. Charley walked about the camp, bathed in the river, washed out his clothes and borrowed a pair of scissors from old John Edmonson to trim his lengthening hair. In his reflection on the river surface he could see that his shoulders had toughened up, his arms had thickened, his face had burned brown and his hair was sun-bleached; he looked a decade older than his years.

For a time he was full of the camp's spreading optimism. They had conquered the clutching sands of the dune country; they were like invincible men. But there were signs to make him wary. Bill Randolph, always willing to fight, lunged around camp in an impatient temper. The strange youth, Carl Chapin, was now and then to be seen threading the trees by himself, eyes vacant; at meals he was silent, moody, sulky—he seemed irritated whenever anyone invaded his privacy enough to ask him a simple question. Old John Edmonson had developed a wheeze and a cough that kept him bent over a good deal of the time. His eyes seemed too bright. Captain McDowell came around often, inspecting equipment; he rationed out food and supplies with a hoarder's miserliness. Even Norval Douglas, who usually seemed willing enough to let the world go its own way as long as it let him go his, seemed strangely anxious at times, and once jumped irritably at an innocent question Charley asked of him. And Crabb—Crabb plowed through the camp with his hands behind him and his head down, like a man restlessly pacing a floor, trying to fight out the solution to some weighty problem. There were many of them, however, who showed no indications of that same strain—Jim Woods for one; Sus Ainsa and the easygoing Captain Bob Holliday, Lieutenant Will Allen, Dr. Oxley.

Norval Douglas spent two days alone out in the hills somewhere. When he returned it was understood, though he talked little of it, that he had encountered a party of Indians and fought a small skirmish with them. He brought back the carcass of a fat mule deer and that night the company, feasting, was the envy of Companies B and C. The following day, inspired by the yellow-eyed scout's example, a group of men representing all three companies went on a hunting foray, and returned at sundown with a good haul of bobcat, javelina boars, jackrabbit and even a whitetail buck. For Charley, who accompanied that party, it was his first opportunity to make use of the arms with which he had been equipped. His first shot, at a bounding jackrabbit, had gone well wide of its mark. He had settled down on the spot and spent an hour in target practice to accustom himself to the gun. Presently young Carl Chapin had come along, and a strange thing happened.

Chapin reined in and dismounted beside Charley's pony. Looking sickly, his eyes bulging a little from his face, Chapin loosened his cinches and came forward with his own rifle. The first thing he said was, "Don't do it that way—don't close one eye when you shoot. You lose perspective. Keep both eyes open. Here—look." Chapin put his hand on Charley's rifle and moved it so that the stock rode higher against his shoulder.

"Try it that way. Sight on the target. Balance your target on top of the front sight. Now cock the hammer."

A pair of metal clicks, loud in the desert, struck Charley's ears. Chapin said, "Take in a deep breath and let half of it out, then hold your breath. When you're steady on the target, give the trigger a steady squeeze. That way you won't know when she'll go off—and so you won't flinch. Try it."

Charley followed his advice. A corner of his mind stood back and was puzzled by Chapin's sudden sociability. He squinted down the barrel, remembered to open his left eye, drew in his breath, and began to squeeze. Chapin said, "Focus your eye on the front sight, not the target." Charley aimed at a protruding spiny segment of a cholla cactus, and squeezed.

When the rifle went off, it startled him; he jumped, and was sure his jump must have thrown the bullet far off course. But the cholla segment tilted and fell softly to the ground. "I'll be damned," Charley said.

"Just remember to squeeze them off," Chapin said. "You won't have any trouble." He put his own rifle to shoulder and almost without seeming to take aim, he fired. Another piece of cholla split away from the plant and fell. Chapin tilted his powderhorn against the rifle muzzle, patched a lead ball with quick competence, and rammed the charge back to the breech with one swift, firm stroke of the ramrod. Charley had not seen him dig for it, but there was a percussion cap in his palm, which he now pinched over the nipple under the big cupped hammer. Then the pale youth slung the rifle over his back. Charley had hardly found time to unsling his own ramrod.

Down the gully, the cutbank had caved in and there was a brief talus slide. On that loose slope of rock and earth appeared the mule-eared shape of a tall jackrabbit. Charley stood still and watched it. The rabbit, startled, froze. But when Charley lifted his ramrod to seat the bullet, the rabbit wheeled and darted away. He saw it bounce past a cluster of creosote bushes and then it was gone. He cursed and capped the rifle. When he looked at Chapin, the pale youth was looking blankly at the spot where the rabbit had disappeared. He had not touched his gun. Charley said, "Damn it, why didn't you shoot him?"

Chapin shrugged his narrow shoulders, coughed twice and spat a pink stream toward the ground, and turned back toward his horse.

"Wait a minute," Charley said.

"What for?"

"Well," Charley began, and felt awkward. "Thanks for the help."

"Yeah," Chapin said, and went on to his horse. He gathered the reins and climbed into the saddle. Charley watched him ride away toward the hills.

Reflecting on the enigma of this pale and brittle-boned youth, he used up a dozen more slugs in practice, at the end of which he found the cholla pretty well chopped down. Then he hunted around the gully wall for the spent bullets, found six or seven of them, and pocketed the smashed pieces of lead. Later he would melt them down and recast them.

When he returned to camp in the evening with a rabbit dead across his saddle, he saw Chapin riding in from the north. Chapin's saddle was empty of game.

In the morning, well fed and impatient, the expedition broke camp and formed its line, and wound forward like a brown curling snake on a brown earth. It was about forty miles southward to Tinajas Altas, which were a string of nine eroded potholes on the eastern face of a massive rock mountain. Storm waters were stored in these pits, and here the party filled to capacity all its barrels, canteens, and water bags. A horse had fallen ill and been shot, and Norval Douglas had sewn watertight bags out of the hide.

Each man was reduced to one blanket and twenty pounds of baggage. Much of the baggage had been left in trust at the sutler's in Fort Yuma. Here on the desert mules began to give out, and one by one the wagons had to be abandoned. More animals were conscripted to carry packs, so that a good portion of the enlisted personnel were set afoot. Scurvy entered the camp surreptitiously; men fell sick and had to support one another. Spirits dropped rapidly. Infection attacked Chuck Parker's leg; Dr. Oxley was sure he would not lose the limb, but Parker was unable to walk, even on crutches. The next water was still ten miles distant when the final wagon cast a tire; there was no spare left, and for six days Parker and two men stayed behind on the desert, while each day the two men marched forward to get water for the animals and brought it back. Finally Crabb gave the order that stragglers must catch up. Charley was there when they removed the fevered Parker from his wagon bed and suspended him in a stretcher between two horses. They caught up with the main party at Cabesa Priete, midway along the Camino del Diablo, under a blistering March sun. The valleys they traveled—the Lechuguilla, the Tulito—were barren and dry, bounded by sawtooth mountains cut from rock without vegetation on their slopes. Sparse growths of catclaw and ironwood mingled with the scattered cacti. There was no shade anywhere. At night the temperatures dropped by fifty degrees and men shook in their single blankets. Not even coyotes called across this forgotten district. Every night when camp was pitched it was Charley's duty to sweep the area for snakes; in this heat they came out of hibernation early. Finding a snake, he would pinion its head under the curved steel butt strap of his rifle.

Then he would cut the head and rattles off with his knife. Jim Woods amassed a considerable collection of diamondback and sidewinder rattles from Charley's gatherings.

CHAPTER 13

Dave McDowell scratched his red beard and frowned into the fire. It was a smoky, stinking little fire, fed with green creosote and paloverde twigs. He took a sparing sip from his canteen, rolled the tepid stale water around in his mouth, swallowed it down a raw throat, and popped a smooth pebble into his mouth, working it around with his tongue to keep the saliva going. He wished he had his tent. All the tents had been abandoned long ago. The scatter of blanket-rolled bodies was hardly military.

A tall shadow loomed in the night. That was Freeman McKinney, trailed by Bob Holliday. The lieutenants stood back in a knot of idle talk. "The general wants a powwow, Dave," McKinney said.

"All right." He stood up and followed them to the big fire, where Crabb sat on his blanket thoughtfully stroking the length of his brown beard. The general's deep eyes lifted slowly to acknowledge them. "Pull up some chairs, gentlemen," he said drily.

McDowell sat down between Holliday and McKinney. McKinney's bald head glistened in the firelight. Back in the semi-shadow stood the constantly vigilant shape of Norval Douglas. "I'm sorry I can't offer you a drink of wine," Crabb said. "Gentlemen, we are faced with a difficult problem."

McDowell looked around. The whole contingent of officers was present. He nodded to Oxley and Will Allen, Quarles and Porter, Colonel McCoun, Johns and Nat Wood. He saw Bob Holliday stretch his long legs toward the fire. Across the blaze, Sus Ainsa looked on with sleepy eyes. "Sick men are becoming a burden to us," Crabb said. "I don't mean that in an unkind way. I'm sure Mr. Douglas will confirm what I have to say." He looked up as if seeking agreement. In the shadows, Norval Douglas's eyes glittered in frosty reflection of the fire.

"The fact is, there is not enough water between here and the town of Sonoyta to sustain us if we continue at our present rate," Crabb said. "I daresay we're hardly making twenty miles a day. This is a grueling country to get across—we knew that when we set out. But frankly I didn't count on having to abandon the wagons and having to lose so many mules and horses along the way. We have reached a point where we will again have to ration water, as we did on the sand dunes west of the Colorado. Gentlemen, I am sure you'll all agree that we do not propose to leave our bones to bleach on this desert along with the others that we see every mile of the way.

"There are almost a score of men," he continued, "who are unfit for forced marches. I refer to every condition from blistered feet to scurvy, and of course the wounded man—what was his name?"

"Parker," said McDowell.

"Yes. Parker. The man needs rest and good food more than anything else, I understand. He can't get either of them here, but by the same token I doubt he's in fit condition to ram forward full-tilt across the desert to Sonoyta. Am I correct, Doctor?"

Oxley nodded. "Indubitably," he muttered. "Indubitably, Henry." Oxley was a strange little man but a good surgeon.

Crabb nodded slowly and an interval passed during which no one spoke. Perhaps Crabb had sunk into one of his odd reveries. But in a moment he lifted his head and seemed to shake himself. He said, "Ah, yes."

McCoun, who, being a colonel, was at least titularly the second in command, spoke in his customary brusque manner: "What do you propose we do about it?"

"Divide the party," Crabb replied. "I suggest we leave an officer behind in charge of the sick. That group can stay behind, rest a bit, and come on to Sonoyta at their own pace. The rest of us will leave as much water and food behind as we dare, and make a forced march to Sonoyta. There we can wait for the others to come up. It's my feeling, gentlemen, that it's that or imperil the entire command."

"It's a risk," Oxley said immediately. "We have no guarantee that the sick men will benefit by a few days' rest. They may be less able to travel later than they are now."

"That's true enough," Crabb said, "but it endangers the rest of us if we all must accommodate ourselves to the pace of the slowest man. I'm convinced we stand a better chance if we divide the regiment."

"What about Indians?" McDowell said. "Wouldn't we be laying the sick men open to an attack?"

Norval Douglas drawled from the shadows; he seemed reluctant to come closer to the fire. "Papagos," he said. "They won't bother anyone. It's too far west for Apaches."

"I'm glad you seem so positive," McDowell told him. Douglas made no answer. His expression was unreadable; only his eyes were clearly visible. McDowell, who had come around to a certain way of thinking in the past few weeks and had for a time reasoned himself into being satisfied with the state of affairs as they were, now felt the returning pressure of uncertain fears.

"I think," Crabb said, "that it would be wise to call for a volunteer. I'm reluctant to order any officer to take on the job of handling these sick men."

That was the trouble, McDowell thought. Crabb was altogether too reluctant. What would happen if, as commander, he came against a situation that called for a bitter decision? McDowell worried about Crabb's indecisiveness; Crabb lacked the fine line of decision that marked a militarily trained man. To have a hedging man in command might well lead to disaster.

"Will anyone offer himself?" Crabb asked.

"I'll stay with them," McKinney said. "I could use a day or two of rest myself."

"Very well. In the morning you'll take Dr. Oxley with you, and make an inspection. The doctor will select those men who are unfit for arduous travel. I anticipate you'll probably find yourself with about eighteen or twenty men on your hands.

107

You'll instruct Lieutenant Henry to take over your company in your absence."

"Good enough," McKinney said, and stood up. "Is that all?"

"Yes. Good luck to you. We'll expect you to arrive in Sonoyta a few days behind us."

"I'll come along as quickly as I can," McKinney said.

The meeting broke up shortly thereafter, and on his way back to his own fire McDowell found that he had the company of Bob Holliday at his shoulder. Holliday swung along with lanky, loping strides, rolling his shoulders as he walked. His hands were rammed inside his waistband and he said, "I see what you mean about the general. He should have given a flat order. You don't call for volunteers in country like this."

They reached the fire. McDowell shared his pipe tobacco with Holliday. The crescent moon appeared, tipped up on one point. Holliday said, "When we came across Arizona ten years ago, we skirted this desert to the north."

"The Mormon Battalion?"

"Yes. It doesn't seem so long ago. Cooke was a good officer. I wonder what happened to him?"

"He wrote a manual on cavalry tactics. Quite good."

"I'd like to see it sometime," Holliday said. "It's hard to believe that stagecoaches go over that trail every day. Ten years ago we broke the trail for the first time. This is a hell of a country. Sometimes I ask myself what the devil I'm doing here."

"One day follows the next," McDowell said. "Eventually you die." He was in a dark mood. "I wonder what made McKinney volunteer?"

"He's an old friend of the general's. I expect he thinks he's doing the general a favor."

"He's going to have a rough time of it. The desert's getting hotter every day."

*   *   *

In this part of Mexico, the sun of late March was an angry god. José Maria Giron, colonel of the governor's troops, felt its malicious arrows against the back of his sweat-damp shirt as he ascended the stone steps of the Governor's Palace of Ures. A sentry came to attention, presenting his rifle, but for the moment Giron ignored the man and let him stand at stiff attention. Giron turned and put his eye on the town. Sun had baked the weathered 'dobes into the land's common yellow gray. Beyond the square he saw the dome of the church. Absently he crossed himself—forehead, shoulder and shoulder, chest. He tipped back his duck-billed hat and hooked a thumb inside the belt strap that glistened as a black ribbon diagonally across his body from shoulder to waist. The air was very hot; a residue of dust hung suspended. He turned, met the utterly blank stare of the sentry, and saluted, whereupon the sentry resumed his legs-apart position at parade rest. Giron went into the shade of the entranceway. A soldier took his hat and sword and, wiping his hands together, Giron turned up the stairs.

At the head of the staircase another sentry barred his way. This man, following orders, demanded and received Giron's papers, though he was an old soldier and Giron had known him for years. Giron took his papers back and spoke a few pleasantries with the soldier, inquiring after his family; and went down the hall.

Beside a wooden statue of Santa Maria stood Ignacio Pesquiera. Aguilar, who was governor at least in name, sat behind the massive oaken desk. Clustered by the far window of the office were Gabilondo and Lorenzo Rodriguez and Jesús Ojeda, the latter two men being officers under Giron's command. Giron nodded to them all and stood waiting with inbred patience, reflecting on the pleasant company of the melon-breasted girl he had been forced to leave behind in his quarters when Pesquiera's message had come. He put a hand on his paunch and pushed it inward. *I am becoming a soft man of middle age,* he thought regretfully. He regarded the stocky, powerful figure of Hilario Gabilondo, who had little fat on him. Gabilondo's arrogant stare met him and made him look away. The taste of beer hung on Giron's tongue.

Pesquiera moved away from the statue and crossed to the governor's desk. He stooped and spoke soft courteous words in Aguilar's ear, whereupon the governor got up and with a certain stiffness left the room. It was unfortunate, Giron thought; no man should have to act as a pawn. Aguilar was no more than Pesquiera's tool. Soon he would be dispensed with. It was the way of politics; that much Giron understood. He knew little of the meaning of politics, and disliked what he had seen of it. He was a soldier.

"Señores," Pesquiera said, and stood by a corner of the desk until the four men had turned toward him. "I have a mission for you."

Giron looked upon his commander expectantly. By the window, Gabilondo cocked his hip against the sash and sat tilted that way, arms folded across his chest. There was something cold in the man's eyes that made a chill run down Giron's back. He was not ordinarily a particularly perceptive man, but it would have been hard to miss the chilly contempt with which Gabilondo looked on everything indiscriminately. Just now that half-lidded gaze was directed at Pesquiera, who seemed to take no notice of it. His gray beard was carefully combed; he wore the clean dark clothes of a *don*. He seemed to be gathering his thoughts. Presently he said:

"My friends, we now have power firmly in our grasp. But to keep it, we must remain popular. Gandara lost office for one reason only. It was not because he was ruthless. It was not because he was greedy. It was, simply, because he lost favor with the people. You understand?"

It was a rhetorical question; no one answered him. He went on:

"The people are happy with us. We must keep them so."

Giron said, "What must we do?"

"Stop the filibusters," Pesquiera said promptly. He was looking at no one in particular.

Giron stiffened. When he looked at Gabilondo, all he could see was the hint of a smile. Pesquiera said in a conversational voice, "My agents have been among the people. We have made it known to the people that Manuel Gandara was responsible for inviting the *Norteamericano* colonists. The people understandably do not wish another Texas."

Pesquiera looked very complacent. Giron wondered about it. He wondered how such a good man could utter such things with so straight a face. He wondered if this was what would happen with others of Pesquiera's promises. But it was politics, and since he did not understand politics, he said nothing.

Pesquiera went on:

"Gandara is to blame, then. The people do not want us to allow the filibusters to invade our state. Señor Crabb must be stopped."

Giron felt the stale taste of beer; he swallowed; he said in a small voice, "How?"

"I have dispatched a messenger with a letter to Sonoyta, which is on the border of the *Estados Unidos*. In the letter I have warned Señor Crabb that we have no further need of his services, and that he would be well advised to turn back."

Giron felt himself relaxing. "That is good," he said, and nodded his head wisely.

"But," Pesquiera continued mildly, "I do not believe that the letter will have much influence on our friend the good Señor Crabb. If you will pardon my saying it, I believe the man is a foolhardy adventurer. Of course, he may take heed. He may turn back. In that case we have nothing to worry about, no? But we must of course be prepared for whatever comes."

He went around the desk and sat down in Aguilar's chair, the governor's seat. The desk top was a massive brown polished surface against which he placed both hands. He sat back with a proprietary air. Giron, standing twenty feet away, folded his hands behind him and tucked his chin down. Pesquiera said: "We must be prepared. All we know for certain is that Crabb left San Francisco in January with approximately one hundred men. How many men he has now, we do not know. He may perhaps have recruited many more soldiers during his journey. He will be made bold because he undoubtedly still expects his comrade, General Cosby, to reinforce him at the Concepcion with one thousand men. I am sure Señor Crabb does not know that General Cosby died five weeks ago in a runaway wagon. An auspicious accident. At any rate, we do not know where

Crabb is now, or how many followers he has. We must assume the worst. Ojeda."

"*Sí*," said Jesús Ojeda, stepping forward from the window, standing smartly at attention. Ojeda wore his sword, Giron noticed. Pesquiera said, "Ojeda, you will take twenty men and march to Sonoyta. If Crabb is still there, you will conceal yourselves until he moves. If he turns north and goes away, you will leave him alone. If not—if he advances across the border and seems to be marching this way, you will fortify your men at Sonoyta to prevent his return."

"*Sí*," Ojeda said. Giron met his eyes. Ojeda was a good soldier. Giron liked him.

"If Crabb has already passed Sonoyta," Pesquiera went on, "you will find out which way he went, and act accordingly. If you find him headed toward the Concepcion, you will dispatch a messenger on a fast horse to the town of Caborca, with a message for Colonel Rodriguez, so that he may prepare himself. *Comprende?*"

"*Sí*," Ojeda said a third time.

"Very well. Rodriguez?"

Lorenzo Rodriguez came forward to stand at Ojeda's shoulder. Giron did not like him so well. He thought that Rodriguez was a fool when it came to military work; he did not see with a soldier's eyes.

"Rodriguez," said Pesquiera, "you will leave immediately with a squad of well-armed soldiers, and you will take with you sufficient wagonloads of arms and ammunition to equip the local militia at the town of Caborca. You will prepare the town for a possible invasion, and you will fortify yourself so that, if Crabb's column arrives, you will be able to contain him until reinforcements arrive. Is that understood?"

"*Sí*," Rodriguez said.

"*Bien*. Now, as to you, Hilario."

Gabilondo did not step forward. He maintained his slouched seat in the windowsill. His bleak gaze wandered around the room like a restless horsefly and finally came to rest on his commander. Pesquiera said: "You will take two hundred soldiers and a pack train with weapons and ammunition to arm as many additional volunteers as you are able to gather in the towns between here and the Concepcion. You will take sufficient time to recruit a large party and train them, at least rudimentarily. At the same time you will maintain a steady march toward the Concepcion, and you will throw scouts forward to find out if the Crabb filibusters have penetrated the valley. If they have, you will make contact with them and stop them. You will prepare yourself to engage them in battle if they choose not to surrender."

Gabilondo's smile was cool. Pesquiera said, "Oh, and you, Giron—you will accompany Hilario as his second-in-command. That is all. Good luck to you, amigos."

Outside, on the steps of the palace, Giron thought of the woman who awaited him in his quarters, and the jug of beer yet half full, and he said, "I suppose we will decamp in the morning, eh, General?"

"We will decamp immediately," Gabilondo said flatly. "Gather your equipment and meet me on the parade ground at the barracks. In half an hour, Colonel." Saying no more, Gabilondo went briskly down the steps pulling on his gloves.

Shrugging with regret, Giron squinted toward the afternoon sun and tramped slowly across the dusty square. There were times when one had to forego one's pleasures for the sake of duty.

CHAPTER 14

From the hilltop, Charley looked back across the barren eroded leagues and saw, bright in the morning sun, the little camp a mile away. One man stood on the flats—Captain Freeman McKinney, waving his hat to them, a tiny shape threatened by the vast sweep of the dry flats. Charley kicked aside the whitened skull bone of a mule. The jaw clattered. He went on, tramping pebbles into the earth. In time they were over the far side of the hill and McKinney's little camp was no longer in view. Mc-Kinney had twenty men, sick or blistered; the main party was reduced to fewer than seventy. Charley trudged along in formation beside old John Edmonson. In front of them walked Carl Chapin, who did not talk at all, and one-eyed Sam Kimmel, who had regretfully left Chuck Parker behind. Kimmel appeared to hold himself responsible for the lurch of the ship that had made his gun go off and smash Parker's leg. Perhaps it was right that he should feel so; Charley didn't know. He did know that as far as his own feelings toward Chuck Parker were concerned, there was no regret in him and no particular sympathy for Parker. It was Parker, after all, who had killed the little miner for his poke.

At the head of the column the officers rode horseback. All the other men were now afoot; what horses and mules could be spared were burdened with packs, and the rest of the stock had been left with McKinney for transportation of the sick. Far out ahead of the column a solitary rider appeared occasionally on the horizon. That was Norval Douglas, scouting the trail and leaving markers as he went. A sluggish current of air scorched Charley's dry skin. He pulled his hat forward against the sun that burned his face. His feet, sore a month ago, had toughened up; his legs moved along with an easy rhythm, wasting no motions. On the nearby horizon swells was a spindle tracery of greasewood and yucca stalks. Particles of mica and pyrites in the ground flashed slivers of brilliance against his squinted eyes. Heat pulsed along the ground. Ahead, the violent pattern of the land buckled up in crooked shattered tangles of yellow and brown and gray.

Across the silent air, old Edmonson's voice seemed to jump at him: "I had a talk with our friend Douglas last night. He's a sound man, but I believe he needs something to soften his hardness."

Charley turned an indifferent glance on him. Just now he felt little respect for Edmonson; the past few weeks had given him the impression that Edmonson was always padding around like a dog waiting for scraps. But at times Charley listened with respect to the old carpenter's talk of kindness and unhurried satisfaction with life as it came. In moments like this one he found himself almost torn between the attitudes of Douglas and Edmonson; he seemed to lose his identity and become nothing but a slate on which impressions of other men were printed.

Edmonson bent over his hollow chest and coughed without losing stride. "That's a bad cough," Charley said.

"Just came back to me recently," Edmonson said, and shrugged. "When I was young, each year there would be a doctor who told me I was dying. After a while you learn to ignore things like that. For a dying man I've lived a good span of years."

"Just the same, this would be a hell of a place to die."

"Well," the old man said, with a quizzical turn of his lips, "perhaps you could suggest a good place to die?"

"You know," Charley said by way of an answer, "I don't think you really know what you've bought into. If you did, maybe you wouldn't be here now."

Edmonson walked scuffing the ground with his bootheels. He said, "Putting too much trust in too many people—perhaps that's my great fault. But I've survived through it this far. With luck I'll last a little longer. I don't have much to lose, at any rate. But with you it's a different thing. I should think that of the two of us, you're the one who's putting the most in the balance."

"I can look out for myself," Charley said.

"That's fine," the old man answered, and Charley wondered if he imagined the touch of dryness on his tone. Hard bright heat lay across the desert. Edmonson gestured with a lunge of his arm. "Just the same," he said, "this is a hell of a thing to die for."

"The desert, you mean?"

"Yes."

"Then what are you doing here?" he said bluntly.

Edmonson looked at him. An obscure smile came to his mouth. "Well, I'll tell you something," he said. "Essentially, nothing has much meaning to an old man. Everything can be canceled at any time. I just walk along and run my little shoestring life and mind my own business most of the time. I like the desert air—even if it's hot I can breathe it. I'm all right, you see, as long as I keep my lungs dry." He paused. There was the sound of feet regularly crunching the earth. Back along the column somewhere a man was softly humming a tune. Edmonson seemed to be rummaging in his thoughts. He said, "You strike me as a shrewd enough young fellow. What are you looking for?"

"Looking for?"

"You must be searching for something. Otherwise why are you here?"

Charley made no answer. In truth, he didn't have a ready answer. "You're still walking around looking for a place to sit down," Edmonson said.

"What's that supposed to mean?"

"When you accumulate a little humility," the old man went on, as if Charley had said nothing, "then perhaps you'll have found what you're looking for. But it will take time. Humility is not a virtue of youth."

"What have I got to be humble about?"

"Exactly," Edmonson murmured. "Youth is arrogance. From where you stand, a man is either a hammer or an anvil. To your eyes there's no third alternative. Therefore, naturally, you seek to become a hammer. Nobody wants to be hammered upon. But you'll be making a great mistake if you maintain that attitude very long."

"Why?"

"You become too hidebound. If you insist on being the hammer, it can only lead you in one direction. You'll become a strong man but a lonely one. Look at Norval Douglas."

"What's wrong with him?"

"He's not a happy man."

"Show me a happy man," Charley said.

"I put myself on display," answered the old man.

Charley could not agree. To reduce oneself to the point of accepting whatever happened—that was not happiness; it was vegetation. Edmonson went on: "When you learn to be con-

116

tent with yourself, you'll have arrived where you wanted to be. Until then, impatience will drive you relentlessly. Look at the way it drives Douglas. He's a strong man, smart. Probably he's never knuckled under in his life. But he's no longer young—and he's still driving himself because he isn't satisfied."

"No," Charley said. "You're wrong. He's satisfied. That's why he pushes himself. The only way to keep your self-respect is to make the most of yourself."

Edmonson chuckled softly; the chuckle turned into a cough. "You've been listening to Douglas too much. All he's really managed to do is find a shortcut from nowhere to nowhere. What will all his driving amount to when he dies?"

"It won't matter then."

"Just so. Then why not be satisfied with things as they are?"

"Because it matters now." Charley said nothing further. He did not, however, believe the old man. He did not see how it could be worthwhile to let the wind push him around until he died. What was important was the now—otherwise the only thing that came after birth was death, and there was no point in living at all. He had learned that much: that the present was no longer a dismal uncertain gray; it was, in fact, the only sure thing he had.

Edmonson, he felt, was an old man who was not so much embittered as unknowingly defeated. The old man had given up, and was now busy trying to convince himself that he had been right in giving up. But it would not suit Charley. The greatest failure of all would be failure for the want of trying. In this old man it seemed that fear had turned to a flame that had consumed his strength. But that was no good. Time was here to be used; it was here for him to make something of it. The words, passing through his mind, seemed to echo something he had heard Norval Douglas say. He could not place the time or memory.

Rich light streamed across the desert. On the hour the column halted to rest. Charley sat down on a flat smooth rock and sipped from his belt canteen. The rifle, slung across his shoulder, was a half-forgotten weight that had worn a callus along his flesh. He laid it aside and pushed his hat back, feeling the wind cut through the dampness of his hair. When he looked at John Edmonson, who was lying back on one elbow and regarding the desert without much interest, it became plain enough that the sharp savor of life had passed the old man by. Charley resolved not to let that happen to him. Probably long ago Edmonson had found himself struggling under the belief, encouraged by his doctors, that life was tragically brief and therefore essentially without value. He had lost his capacity to believe; he had flattened himself and somewhere he had obviously lost the knowledge that the day was a stretch of time that he could use as a tool to his accomplishment.

The earth glittered. A peak stood round and lofty, its slopes darkened by rock. The air was thin and at the same time like a fire's radiant heat, with an acid burn against the skin. Dust gritted on the roof of his mouth. When he turned his head, the shirt collar scraped his neck. At the head of the column, Colonel McCoun made a signal and the men climbed to their feet. Charley capped his canteen, hung the rifle across his shoulder, and stepped into line.

*   *   *

A few trees; a patternless scatter of adobe buildings, made with great thick walls and tiny windows. A cupola-roofed well in the center of the square. One cactus wren perched with dusty weariness on the rim of the well. A heavy woman in a shapeless dress, black dusty hair knotted and stringy across her eyes, moving on springless feet with a wooden bucket toward the well; the bird flapped its wings and departed for a slim mesquite branch at the edge of the square. The woman reached the well and listlessly brought up the bucket on its rope, and balanced it on her head when she trudged back into the shade of her house. Across the square on the veranda of his office sat the *alcalde*, whose name was Redondo, and who was also the *comisario* of Sonoyta —behind him his building served as general store, mayor's office, jail. Sonoyta was technically north of the border, and thus a part of the newly annexed Gadsden Purchase area of Arizona; but Redondo, who had lived here under Spanish and Mexican flags, was a man slow to heed change, and still owed his allegiance to Mexico—in particular, to the governor of Sonora. Perhaps it was a trifle illegal; but no representative of the United States, or of the Territory of Arizona, had ever paid a call on him, and in the absence of orders to the contrary, Redondo considered himself a Mexican subject. He looked upon his town without delusions. No one cared very much, one way or another, what happened in Sonoyta. The surveyors had been haphazard, lazy men, and perhaps after all it was true that if a decent survey of the boundary had been made, Sonoyta might perhaps still remain a part of Sonora. But Sonora did not seem to care, and Arizona remained silent, and for all practical purposes Sonoyta town was a reasonably independent province by itself, and Redondo its baron. He was satisfied.

He was a potbellied man of middle years, with no particular distinction of features except for a scar along his cheek that he had earned at San Jacinto in the war against Texas. He wore it as a badge of honor. Not all men could claim to have fought under the great general, Santa Anna. Redondo had a habit of running his index fingernail along the ridge of the scar.

His wife, who had put on weight in the past few years, came from the store and spoke a few words to him and dipped a drink of water for herself out of the *olla*, the clay jug that hung under the veranda roof suspended in a net of rope. Having satisfied her thirst, she replaced the long-handled dipper in the *olla* and made her brown-skinned, heavy-legged way back inside the store. Redondo remained seated in his cane-bottom chair; it was too hot to busy himself. He thought without emotion that the summer would get a good deal hotter before it got cooler. Today was only the twenty-seventh of March. The thermometer hung above him and he had to twist his head to look at it; bunched folds of fat rippled along his neck. Ninety-six degrees in the shade. He poked a cheroot in his mouth and struck flame with a flint-and-steel mechanism, and thought that in another two months the midday temperature would be up to a hundred and fifteen. Sometimes it gave him cause to wonder why humanity sought out such inclement districts in which to build homes. Why had anyone ever come here? The nearest town of any consequence was Altar, in Sonora on the Concepcion, and that was almost two hundred kilometers distant. To the northeast, it was even farther to Tubac and Tucson. He made no sense of it. For himself, he would never have settled here, except that the government had made him *alcalde*, and as the only storekeeper except for Dunbar within forty miles in any direction he was bound to make a profit.

His daughter Teresa appeared in the doorway and he made a frown at her, so that she shut the door to keep the heat out. She dipped a drink from the *olla* and handed the cup to him. He muttered his thanks and drank, and handed the cup back. Teresa drank the rest of the cupful. "It is very hot," she said.

"It will get worse."

"Of course." Teresa put the cup back into the *olla*. Redondo took pride in his daughter. Her back was straight, her waist was long and slim. Her eyes and hair glistened like a raven's wing. Her flesh was smooth and brown; her arms were firmly round. She was a very fine daughter. He hoped to see her marry a wealthy man. There was a *ranchero* from San Perfecto who had been calling on her of late. He was not an old man yet—he was only thirty-one—and he owned a great many acres and many head of cattle. Unfortunately he was quite fat; but one could not ask for everything. The *ranchero* was a good suitor. Even so, Redondo now and then wished idly that he could live in a larger town, so that his daughter would have more to choose from.

She had a small head, set aristocratically on a long graceful neck. When he considered his own bull-throat and meaty shoulders, he was amazed that she had proved so beautiful. He wore a gun at his hip, not so much because he was the only law officer within three days' ride, but rather to keep the young *caballeros* aware that his daughter Teresa was not to be trifled with. She was but sixteen. There was plenty of time yet.

She was nibbling on a salt cracker; her hip was perched against one of the posts that supported the veranda roof. Since his was the only shaded porch in Sonoyta, Redondo was jealously proud of it. He squinted into the west and tried to decide whether it would rain. There had been no rain for three months. There were gray clouds on the western horizon, but on the other hand there was no particular wind; and in all his experience he had never known it to rain without raising a wind first.

A horseman trotted into town from the northwest. That was young Luis, and since Luis was something of a young rake, Redondo told his daughter to go inside the store. She went, after casting an innocent but speculative look toward the slim rider. Luis rode up, his horse's hoofs boiling up little whorls of dust, and dismounted gracefully, leaving the reins trailing and coming up on the porch with a tinkle of spurs. Luis grinned amiably and touched his thin black mustache, and dipped a drink for himself out of the *olla*. "*Muy seco*," he said—very dry. After wiping his lips he said, "There is a very large group of gringos approaching from that way." He waved a hand.

"How large?"

"Many more than I could count on fingers and toes," said Luis. "Most are on foot. A few ride horses. They have a number of pack animals, both horses and mules."

"They are armed?"

Luis gave him an impatient look. "What kind of question is this? Only a fool empty in the head would travel in this country without arms. Of course they are armed."

Redondo for the moment chose to ignore the young man's sass. "Anything more?"

"They will be here within two hours, I think."

"Good. Thank you, Luis."

Luis grinned and stepped off the porch, and led his horse out into the square. His spurs dragged the dust. He pulled up a bucket of water at the well and gave his horse a drink, then loosened the cinch and led the horse out of the square toward his father's stable. Redondo watched him go. The party Luis had reported would no doubt be the *Norteamericano* filibusters against whom Pesquiera's dispatch rider had warned him not a week past.

He sighed; his wide chest lifted and fell. In a moment he went inside the store and around behind the counter, where he brought out a double-barreled shotgun. He inspected its loads, gave wife and daughter a bleak look, and returned to the porch. When he sat down he put the shotgun across his lap.

Time stretched at a ragged pace. Teresa came out for another drink of water, and he said to her, "I have instructions for you, *niña*. There is a crowd of gringo pirates on the road coming here. They will arrive within an hour—if you look closely you can see their dust beyond the bald mountain."

She looked. "I see nothing, *Papa*."

"Just the same, the pirates are there. I do not wish you to be visible to them. One does not put temptation in the devil's path. I have decided what you must do."

"*Sí, Papa?*"

"Go down to your Aunt Lita's house by the arroyo. Stay there with her until the gringos have left the town."

"All right," she said.

"Take a gift for your aunt from the store. And take food with you. The gringos may stay here for an hour or a week—I do not know. You are to avoid them at all times. Do not speak to any of them. Keep a knife with you. *Comprendes?*"

"*Sí, Papa.*"

"Go, then."

She turned into the store. On his cane-bottom chair, Redondo touched the hot metal of the shotgun and settled back to wait. The dust haze to the northwest was advancing slowly. The thermometer read ninety-seven degrees.

CHAPTER 15

It was Sus Ainsa's feeling that matters were not as they should be. Normally he was easygoing enough, in most respects, to take adversity as it came. Today it had come in the form of a complacently delivered message uttered by the fat *alcalde* of the town, Redondo. The message had been brief and to the point. It had taken Redondo approximately a minute and a half to speak it. It was now taking the rest of the afternoon to digest it.

The column was encamped in the scanty shade of a row of mesquites that bordered the rim of a dry eroded creek, an arroyo. Crabb was seated with his back against the bole of one such tree. It was so stunted that its branches barely left his face visible. Sus squatted on the dusty ground and, with the other officers, looked worried. The sun was made of brass; its great brilliance attempted to fry them all. Sus's shirt was soaked against his back and there were drops of oil sweat on his forehead. A lean man, he did not normally perspire much. His legs felt cramped and he stood up to stretch them. He looked out across the camp at men feeding horses, men playing cards, men oiling guns, men arranging equipment, men talking in quiet little knots of conversation.

Sus thought back upon the *alcalde*, stuffed with self-importance, sitting in his cane-bottom chair on the porch and delivering his message with pompous tones. "The government of Governor Aguilar has instructed me to inform Señor H. A. Crabb and his party that the people of Mexico will tolerate no invasion. The administration of Governor Aguilar accepts no responsibility for treasonous or unlawful pacts entered into by any previous administration. The present administration refuses to honor any such pacts, and accordingly announces to all immigrants or attempted invaders that to enter upon Mexican sovereign soil is to risk property and even life. No covenants that lead to invasion will be honored. I speak with the authority of the Señor Don José de Aguilar, Governor by God's Grace of the State of Sonora."

The *alcalde* had gestured for emphasis with the black shotgun he held securely. Then Crabb had replied to him that the party would make camp outside town while considering the announcement. Redondo had nodded and smiled and told them to take all the time they desired. Crabb had been steaming when they reached the campsite, and Captain David McDowell had threatened to return to town and wring Redondo's fat neck.

Crabb began to talk, slowly at first, then with heat. "The message is clear enough. Pesquiera, through his puppet Aguilar, has made it plain that he's going back on his word. This is what we all feared when we learned that Pesquiera had whipped Gandara. Frankly I had hopes that Pesquiera would prove to be an honorable man and would keep faith with his contracts in spite of the fact that he no longer needed the services we were supposed to supply. After all, as you gentlemen know, Pesquiera is related to my wife, and I had hoped that would count for something. It's clear now, however, that not only is Pesquiera going back on his word, he's actually denying that he ever gave his word. From the wording of the threat Redondo gave us, it's plain that Pesquiera is trying to shift the blame to Gandara. That's what he meant by saying he would not honor any pacts made by 'previous administrations.' Of course it's hogwash, but the Mexican people will believe it. They'll believe anything Pesquiera tells them. They're fools—cattle. They don't deserve sovereignty over this country. Look at the kind of backbiting men who are their leaders. Look at Pesquiera—a man entirely without honor. Gentlemen, I believe that whatever else happens, the people of Sonora should at least be rescued from such foul dealers as Pesquiera and his followers."

Sus found himself smiling a little. It was typical of Crabb, to get confounded in his own rhetoric so that at one moment he condemned the people as cattle, and at the next moment he vowed that they deserved to be rescued from their leaders.

"Gentlemen," Crabb said, "my friends. We have come far. The desert lies behind us. We have experienced many a hardship. If we allow ourselves to be intimidated and driven away by this pompous threat, then what is it all to come to? Have we labored in vain? I know that some of you fought in the war against Mexico not a decade past. You know the qualities of the Mexican fighting man. Without intending offense to my fine brother-in-law here"—Sus had to smile again—"I think we must all agree that as a soldier, the Mexican makes a very poor showing for himself. Gentlemen, I believe we have come too far to be turned back now. I believe we have expended too much money, too much effort, and too much time to allow ourselves to fail in the face of an empty threat. My friends"—and here his voice rose to a fine peak of energy—"I am convinced that together we must resolve to advance!"

It was McCoun who offered objection. Colonel W. H. McCoun. Sus looked upon the man with a certain measure of cool contempt. McCoun had been a well-known leader in the state legislature for many years. He had held the respect and friendship of his constituents in the palm of his hand, until at a late date during the last elections he had switched his allegiance to Crabb and the Know-Nothings. And now McCoun gnawed the political bone that had been tossed to him—the position of second-in-command of the expedition. Sus had never liked the big, balloon-cheeked man; he liked him even less now for his hedging.

"It's a nice speech, Henry," McCoun said. "I applaud you. You have a knack of uttering the proper words of courage. But I'm not sure that this is the time for courage or rashness. After all, our skins hang in the balance."

Crabb said quietly, "I'm disappointed in you, old friend."

"If you want to despise me for cowardice, go ahead," McCoun said. "But believe me, if mine were the only life I had to consider, I'd probably be a good deal bolder. As it is, I don't find it as easy as you seem to find it. In effect you're asking eighty or ninety men to march into a situation that we know is a hostile one. Even under the best of possible circumstances, men are bound to be hurt or killed."

"You seem to forget," Crabb told him, "that within a week's time General Cosby will be on the Concepcion with a thousand troops. We have promised to meet him in the Altar valley. What is he to do if we don't arrive?"

"I'm forgetting nothing," McCoun said. "Send a dispatch rider to meet Cosby farther downriver. Tell him to turn back, if there's still time for it."

"And if there isn't? My friend, by this time Cosby has undoubtedly landed his force at Lobos Bay. If Pesquiera is looking for an armed invasion, he's already got one. You don't think we could stop him now, do you?"

"We might be able to turn Cosby back before there's more bloodshed than necessary," McCoun insisted. "Besides, with a thousand men he can take care of himself better than we can."

Crabb looked up toward the mile-distant adobes of Sonoyta, golden in the afternoon sun. Shadows were sharp-edged and olive in color. He was stroking his brown beard—it was, Sus knew, a sign of thoughtfulness. Presently he said, "No. I suspect that if Pesquiera is preparing defenses against us, he will by now have been advised that Cosby's army has made a landing on the western shore. It will be a good opportunity for us to move down the Concepcion and take Altar and Caborca from behind, and reinforce Cosby's column from inland. Gentlemen, the truth of the matter is that we stand in a good strategic position. I don't understand this talk of retreat. If Pesquiera has alerted his troops, so much the better—we shall catch him where he's not expecting it."

Sus watched him with interest. This was almost a new Crabb —resolute, belligerent, offensive. He suspected that Pesquiera's brusque threat had piqued Crabb to the point of stubborn resistance and retaliation.

"I want to hear no more arguments," Crabb said. "We will advance as planned."

McCoun, a politician, was unwilling to take orders flatly without response. He continued his argument, but failed to sway Crabb. Sus watched it all with dry amusement and a growing concern. His own principal objective in this affair was to restore his family to its proper place in the Sonoran hierarchy. The revolution years ago had stripped the Ainsa clan of its mines and lands and driven them out of Mexico. Displaced to San Francisco, they had done well; but it was a needle pricking the family pride that their lost properties in the Arizpe district had never been restored to them. Sus had seen, in the alliance between Crabb and Pesquiera—both of them relatives—a good chance to effect such a restoration of property and position. But now he could see easily enough that if Pesquiera had turned against

Crabb in spite of his promise, then he would just as quickly turn against the Ainsa family in spite of his promise to them. It seemed clear enough to Sus that if he were to turn back now, he would have exhausted himself for nothing. Crabb was right. No doubt the general was exaggerating the ineffectiveness of Mexican soldiery, but at the same time Sus was confident that with Cosby's force on the mainland, victory was a distinct possibility. For himself he was willing to take the risks; as for the other men, it was not up to him to decide for them.

The meeting broke up in the late afternoon. McCoun went away disgruntled and dissatisfied. Holliday and McDowell left together, talking together with evident concern. The other officers drifted back to their companies and in a short while, with the sun half an hour above the horizon, Sus found himself alone with Crabb. Crabb nodded to him and said, "Get out a pen and some paper, Sus. I want to dictate a letter to you. You'll translate it into Spanish."

Sus walked across a part of the camp to get to his traveling bag. Inside he found a quill pen, a sheaf of paper, an ink jar. He took these back with him toward Crabb. On the way he heard men talking earnestly among themselves. Word was already out; talk spread fast. An aura of excitement permeated the camp. Sus squatted down and balanced the paper on his knee. He uncapped the inkwell, dipped the pen, and said, "All right."

"Sir," Crabb began, speaking slowly as he thought out his words. "In accordance with the colonization laws of Mexico and with several definite invitations from the most influential citizens of Sonora, I have entered the boundaries of your state with one hundred followers and in advance of many others, expecting to make happy homes among you."

Sus wrote quickly: *"De conformidad con las leyes de la Colonización de México . . ."* When he finished he looked up.

Crabb went on:

"I have come with the intention of hurting no one, with no intrigues either public or private."

Sus smiled but kept writing.

"Since my arrival," Crabb said, "I have given no indication of evil designs, but on the contrary I have made peaceful overtures. It is true that I am equipped with weapons and powder, but you will know that it is not customary for Americans or any other civilized people to travel without them; furthermore we are about to travel where the Apache Indians are always committing depredations."

Sus wrote busily, now and then chewing the quill while he chose a word. Once he said, "Wait one minute, *hermano*," and caught up. "All right," he said. "Go on from there."

"But bear in mind, sir," Crabb said, "whatever we may be forced to endure shall fall on the heads of you and your followers."

"Let us pray," Sus murmured while he wrote. The sun was dropping into the clouds to the west. The sky grew dim and Sus had to bend over his writing.

Crabb went on dictating: "I have come to your land because I have the right to come, as I have shown, expecting to be greeted with open arms; but now I see that I am to meet death among enemies who are destitute of decency. I protest against any hostile act toward my companions here and about to arrive. You have your own path to follow, but keep this in mind: should blood be shed, it will be on your head, and not on mine. Nonetheless you are free to proceed with your evil preparations. As for me, I shall lose no time in advancing to the place where I have intended to go for some time, and I am now only awaiting my party. I am the leader and my intention is to obey the dictates of the laws of self-preservation and nature."

Crabb nodded. "Close it and I'll affix my signature."

When the letter was sealed, Crabb said, "Give it to this town warden—what's his name?"

"Redondo."

"Yes. I wonder if he's related to the Redondo who's the prefect of the Altar district? At any rate, give the letter to him and have him send it without delay. Give him some money to pay a messenger."

"I think," Sus suggested, "that this letter will not be received with great joy."

"I've stated my position," Crabb answered. "In view of that, they can hardly claim we invaded them under false pretenses, or that we sneaked up on them. The letter will give us a certain measure of protection if any of this ever comes to court."

"I suppose it will," Sus admitted. "But I get the feeling that Pesquiera and his crew of cutthroats—Gabilondo and the rest—are not of the sort to be inclined toward courtroom victories."

"Just the same, it covers us from one direction, and states our intent plainly enough."

"Perhaps it does." Sus got up, feeling the taut bunching of his leg muscles, and turned away into the gathering twilight.

In town, he gave up the letter to Redondo and made every effort to impress the slow, fat *alcalde* that the letter must be delivered without delay. Redondo displayed no reaction until Sus produced a number of gold coins, whereupon Redondo's eyes opened a little wider and he nodded, promising to see to it that the letter was dispatched in haste. Redondo went to the door, swept the plaza with his gaze, and expanded his chest to shout: "Luis!"

A young man with a thin black mustache came up from the well, spurs making small sounds in the dusk. "*Sí, jefe?*"

Redondo handed him the letter, mentioned the name and address of the officer to whom it was to be delivered for transfer into the governor's hands, and put coins in the young man's palm. Sus had to grin when he saw that the number of coins Redondo gave to Luis was not the same number of coins that Sus had given to the *alcalde*. Redondo said briskly, "Ride immediately, Luis. The message is important. You can change horses at San Perfecto and Soquete."

"*Sí, jefe,*" Luis said, and strode away toward the stable.

Redondo turned to Sus and nodded. "The letter will be delivered with all possible haste, señor."

"*Mil gracias,*" Sus murmured, and went outside. Clouds still hung tantalizingly on the western rim of the earth; they did not seem to have advanced at all. Sus thought with anticipatory pleasure of the possibility of rain—rain to cool the air, to cleanse it, to muffle the stinging dust and pack the ground hard.

When he arrived back in camp, Crabb was eating by himself under the shade of the mesquite tree so that he was hardly visible in the deep shadows there. Crabb had saved an extra plate; Sus sat down to eat with him. The clouds were painted brilliant shades of crimson and yellow. As he watched and ate, they dimmed visibly, and by the time his plate was emptied the only hue still distinguishable in the west was a paling pink that soon disappeared. He thought with amusement of the fat, self-important *alcalde* who seemed so busy trying to please all sides at once. He took Crabb's utensils and his own, and scrubbed them clean with sand before he turned them in to the kitchen detail. When he was walking back to Crabb, he saw Norval Douglas sitting off by himself in the shadows smoking a pipe. Douglas's hatbrim rose, indicating his interest in Sus, and Sus waved. Douglas nodded and kept his solitary vigil. A hard and lonely man, Sus reflected.

The stars winked into visibility as a chipped cloudy whitewash on the sky's inverted surface. There was an endlessness about desert nights; the sky, never black, was usually a kind of deep substance of cobalt such as one might see looking into a gemstone or a pool of still water. Crisply traced were the silhouettes of desert brush and cactus. The earth was pale cream in color and stretched away like a stilled ocean. At night there was almost always a gentle wind that brushed cheeks and ears with dry coolness.

When the camp's after-supper chores were done, Crabb called for a meeting. Men built a single fire up until, huge and crimson, it dominated the desert and illuminated a wide area of expectant faces. The entire command stood around in a tightly bunched semicircle. Crabb stood so near the fire that he seemed in danger of being singed; the flames lit up one side of his face and clothing so that he appeared like a strange kind of bearded beast, one-half livid Mephistopheles and the other half a man in shadow. The round jut of his cheek glistened redly. He seemed to have planned it all for a calculated effect. He began to speak, mildly at first, then with increasing energy. Sus stood on the fringe of the companies, hands in his pockets, watching with his customary detached irony, but the power of Crabb's ascending fervor caught him up just as it caught up every soul in the crowd. The general's deep round voice boomed across the plains and slapped against the men like a prodding, searching fist, seeking out the points of leverage from which men's emotions might be turned, pressing gently enough but boosting every man to a peak of enthusiastic spirit. It was, Sus admitted, as inspired a rhetoric as Crabb had ever displayed; it was not colored or dampened by his usual spray of meaningless phrases, nor was it weakened by any of the contradictions with which his speeches had sometimes been hedged. It wheeled and darted, picking out facts and myths and molding them together so that one was indistinguishable from the other. It built, ignited, and fed a fire of resolution and trust—a fire that leaped in men as this great bonfire danced on the desert. It lifted men and made them stretch tall in their boots. It dashed to earth and shattered any residue of uncertainty or reluctance or fear that might have settled in men's hearts. It condemned betrayal and made a scapegoat of Pesquiera; it called for honor and courage and fortitude. It demanded loyalty, and got it. It demanded unconditional affirmation, and got that too. And when Crabb was finished, his eyes gleaming and sweat pouring from his face, his arms finally subsiding, his tongue moistening cracked lips, then the command roared as with the giant voice of one giant man. It was a great cheer that rang across the desert night. And that, Sus knew, was exactly what Crabb had hoped for and calculated toward. He had the men now, as he had never had them before. They were his now; they were in his hands and he could make of them what he wished.

It had to be that way, Sus knew. It was the only way Crabb could maintain the expedition and fling it forward in the face of mounting adversities. After tonight, and for some time to come, men would remember the fire of the flame-painted orator, and no man would question him or the acts of his leadership.

Sus went with Crabb back to the mesquite tree by the arroyo. He spread his blankets and sat down, and saw that Crabb was trembling in all his joints. That much the speech had taken out of him. Crabb borrowed a cigar from him and lit it, and puffed furiously, presently lying back. The cigar shook violently in his fingers; he looked at his hand and smiled. "That was a great moment, Sus. I don't think you know what it can feel like to hold the spirits of threescore men in your palm."

"I think I can get an idea of it," Sus said.

"It was a high point of my life," Crabb said. "I don't think I've ever made a more stunning speech." He grinned; he was like a gleeful child at this moment. He smoked the cigar busily until it grew a tall ash; he flicked the ash away and poked the cigar into a corner of his mouth, and talked slurringly around it. "A fine moment. A fine, fine moment, Sus."

"Yes."

A nocturnal bird, perhaps a cactus owl, flapped by not far overhead. Sus wondered idly if the Evans boy had swept the camp for snakes, as he was supposed to do each night. He saw the outline of Norval Douglas's lean shape stalking the night; Douglas, supremely self-sufficient, was nonetheless a lonely and restless man. Sus wondered what had made the scout choose the kind of life he led. What, for that matter, caused anyone's choice of a course? Was it chance, or will?

"We can't stay here long," Crabb was saying. Sus dragged his mind back and nodded in answer. Crabb said, "If McKinney and his party do not appear within forty-eight hours, we'll have to go on to the Concepcion without them." He paused, and added slowly, "If that happens, I shall leave you behind to tell McKinney to come along after me with all possible haste. Those men who are absolutely unfit to travel will have to remain here. You will stay and watch over them."

"Me?"

"Yes."

Sus frowned. Crabb ground his cigar into the earth with his bootheel. Sus said, "What do you mean? Anyone could stay behind and act as nurse. Why choose me?"

"Because," Crabb said bleakly, "I have a strange feeling about what's ahead of us."

"*Tontería*," Sus said, and swore. "Foolishness."

"No doubt it is. Just the same, you will stay."

"You are ordering me?"

"I am," Crabb said.

"What if I refuse to obey?"

"Do you refuse?" the general countered.

Sus grumbled. "I shall have to think about it."

"Do that," Crabb said. He lay back with his elbows bent, hands under his head and one knee uplifted. Across the camp drifted the wail of the harmonica. "That's a sign of spirit," Crabb said. "I haven't heard that harmonica in weeks. I thought we'd lost it."

"What makes you think my skin is so valuable?" Sus said.

Crabb's answer was a long time coming. The moon appeared with startling abruptness in the east, over the peak called Baboquivari, and spread a pale glow across the desert surface. Presently Crabb spoke. "All the officers in this expedition can be classified into two groups. Unemployed politicians and unemployed soldiers. They joined this expedition out of greed, or out of boredom, or perhaps out of a foolish delusion that by clinging to the tails of my coat they might rise to positions of power in a new state. To a man they possess a single opinion of me: that I am a misguided, disgruntled idealist with vast illusions. Well, so be it. Perhaps I am. At moments I look upon myself as a grand fool. But at least I am a fool with a purpose. I have a dream. I own a great sweep of imagination—I can visualize this continent as it should be, and as it will be one day. All one great nation, from Panama to the Arctic. It is the American destiny. I'm not uttering political stupidities now, Sus. I mean what I say to you. In my lifetime I've spoken many a lie, when I thought it would gain a proper goal. But tonight you have the privilege of hearing an old sour politician give vent to the truth. I have my dreams and, even if they may be unattainable to me, I will at least have given my body and my soul toward the fulfillment of them. That much, my young friend, can be said for none of the others here. Their *cause celebre*, whatever it may be, is a selfish one. Their dreams encompass no more of a scope than can be held in the hand or chalked up in an account book. In short, they deserve whatever befalls them. I refuse to make myself responsible for their folly simply because they have elected to follow my leadership."

Sus allowed a moment of respectful silence to intervene before he said, "All that may be true, *hermano*, although I confess it seems to me that you take a somewhat cynical view of some of our companions. Still, supposing it is true, what makes me any different from the others? Why single me out to remain behind?"

"Because," Crabb said, "you are the only one who means anything to me. Your own dream is not a great one. I know that. You simply hope to restore your family's name to its rightful position of respect, and regain a number of properties in the bargain. Even that much is a more honest end than what the rest of them seek. But the truth is that both of us know you are, underneath all your youthful insolence and lovemaking and good humor, a man of good heart. In truth I'm fond of you, Sus. It's more than I can say for any other man on this trip."

"And so," Sus said, "you choose to leave behind you the only man whose company you enjoy."

"The trip henceforth will be more lonely for me," Crabb conceded.

"Then why leave me here?"

"I'm not in a mood for arguments. Not even friendly ones."

"This is more than a friendly argument, *hermano*."

"Very well," said Crabb. "You wish to know my reason?"

"I do."

"I don't want you to die."

"Do you expect to die?"

"In truth, I don't know what to expect. I know only that I'll feel better if you do as I say, and if you stop questioning my instructions."

"I shall have to think about it," Sus said again, and rolled up in his blankets, troubled and pensive.

CHAPTER 16

Morning; the camp stirred, came alive. It would be a day of waiting. After breakfast old Edmonson sat by his folded blanket
making repairs in a bridle; Charley watched him work.

A roadrunner popped into sight not twenty feet distant and
stood staring alertly at the two men. It was a big bird, almost
two feet long from beak to the long heavy balance of straight tail
feathers. Drab gray shot with streaks of black, it had two bright
spots of color under its eyes. It blinked, cocked its head, and uttered a sound like a pigeon. "That's a strange bird," Edmonson
said. When he spoke the bird hopped away rapidly. "You'd think
on this desert, a bird that couldn't fly wouldn't have a chance."

"They can fly," Charley said.

"Not more than a few yards," Edmonson said. "I've watched
that one all morning. I think he lives here. He's a little angry
with us for squatting on his property. Every few minutes he
comes back to see if we've gone." Edmonson sighed and changed
position. "He's impatient to get rid of us. We're not welcome
here, you see. It gives a man a sad feeling."

Charley shaded his eyes with his hatbrim and swept the camp
with an idle glance. Some men were playing poker in the miserly
shade of a paloverde. By himself on the slope sat Carl Chapin,
against whose young pallid flesh no amount of sun could throw
a tan; Chapin bent over the gun he was cleaning and coughed
once or twice, spitting beside him. The rasp of his cough reached
Charley. General Crabb was at the lip of the arroyo, watching the
camp and stroking his brown beard in thought.

Edmonson put the bridle aside and began to pack his awl and
lacings away in their kit. "That should hold," he said in a satisfied way. He pulled his knees up and wrapped his arms around
them. Charley caught him staring sadly toward the mountain
peaks, hazed in violet distance. Edmonson said, "I was thinking

of the general's speech last night. It's frightening, the effect one man's will can have." The old man patted his pockets. "Have you seen my pipe?"

"No."

"Perhaps I dropped it by the campfire." He got up and walked away, his back a little stooped.

Charley settled back to enjoy the day's ease, but just then a corner of his vision detected movement, and some distance to the west along the bank of the arroyo he saw a tan-gray jackrabbit humping away as though on coil springs. Charley rolled around to reach his rifle, but the rabbit bounded out of sight down into the arroyo.

Hunger for the taste of meat pushed Charley to his feet. He walked to the rim of the cutbank and looked down the gully. Nothing stirred. On the back of his tongue was the aftertaste of the salty jerked beef he had eaten for breakfast today and yesterday and for numberless days before that. He checked the rifle's percussion cap and ran along the lip of the arroyo. The sun was hot on his shirt; the metal of the rifle's lockplate almost seared his hand. The arroyo made a sudden turn, and he saw the rabbit fifty yards down the dry bed, standing in quivering motionlessness, it forepaws raised to cup something on a plant. One long ear twitched, and as Charley sighted his rifle, the rabbit plunged away in great loping bounds. He could hear the *slap-slap* of its big hind feet against the soft sand in the arroyo. It leaped around a further bend; Charley muttered an oath and ran forward.

Budding anger grew in him when the jackrabbit continued to elude him. He followed relentlessly. Every now and then it popped into sight, but dived away before he could take a shot at it. He almost thought it was laughing. Once he had it in his sights and was curling his finger around the trigger when it wheeled behind a scrub and skittered away down the bed of the winding arroyo. Charley's palms began to sweat; as he ran he wiped them, one at a time, against his trousers, swearing bright oaths.

Unwilling to give up, he let the taunting jackrabbit lead him far from camp. He did not know how many miles he had come.

He walked on weary legs and cursed monotonously. The arroyo curled around the end of a sparsely brush-dotted hill. When he rounded that turn he saw, not far ahead, a large clump of trees—cottonwoods, mostly, with smaller mesquites and paloverdes roundabout. The jackrabbit was nowhere in sight.

He sighed and sat down, cuffing his hat back to release the collected sweat under its band. The tips of his hair, where it stuck out from under the hat, were bleached several shades lighter than the rest. He dragged his sleeve across his forehead to mop away sweat. When he looked back, the campsite was out of sight behind the hill he had come around, but the town of Sonoyta was visible across the burning flats—box-shaped 'dobes, their hues weathered into the common bright drabness of the plain. Two or three miles away, he guessed; and that put the camp an equal distance away. It would be a long, dusty walk home, empty-handed. But he did not get up yet. He regretted that he did not have his canteen. He picked up a pebble, rubbed it clean, and sucked on it for a while, but even that did not seem to moisten his dry mouth.

He had another look at the clump of cottonwoods a hundred yards down the arroyo. Where there were trees, there must be water. Of course, the water might be some distance underground, inaccessible. But he was here now and it was worth a try. He got up wearily and was for a moment aware of the unwashed smell of his own body, baking in the sunlight. He trudged along the arroyo bank. When he came nearer the trees, the dry earth on the floor of the arroyo began to turn darker brown in color, an indication of moisture near the surface. A small excitement lifted him. He increased his pace.

Above the cottonwoods, on a little hill, squatted a soilitary building, a small square adobe house with thick walls and small windows. A clothesline ran back from a corner of the house, hung with sun-bleached clothes and pieces of cloth. It was a strangely incongruous scene on the face of the desert wilderness. Charley hesitated, watching the house, but there was no sign of activity there, and he went on into the cool shade of the tall cottonwoods.

For a moment it was like walking out of the sunlight into a dark room. He could make out nothing; his eyes had to accustom themselves to the dimness. The contrast between light and shade was that great on the desert. Presently he threaded a path among the trees and found, in the secluded center of the grove, a small pool. Its slightly steamy odor reached his nostrils. He bent down on its grassy bank. The water seemed reasonably clear; at least it was not stagnant. No doubt the pool was fed by some kind of artesian spring. It was a strange thing to find in such country; here in the depths of the grove the desert flats were almost concealed from sight, and except for the heat of the air, which was diminished by the shade, it would have been easy to believe himself back in the California hills. The water lapped gently near his knees. Since there was no wind, the movement of the water must be due to an underground flow. He cupped his hands and knelt forward, brought a handful of water to his mouth and sipped tentatively. It tasted fresh and clean. He swept off his hat and lay belly-flat on the bank, pushing his face into the water, running the water through his hair, splashing it down under the back of his collar. He kept his face under water until he felt the need to breathe. Then he sat up, and a thought came to him, pulling his lips back in a smile that was both sly and happy.

He got to his feet and walked around the pool, and went up toward the far fringe of the trees until he could see the adobe house. A small breeze came along, cooling his damp hair and face, and a moment later, traveling uphill, it made the hanging garments flap lazily. No one was in view.

Still smiling, Charley turned back to the pool. At its bank he stripped quickly and waded into the center of it. The water was about three feet deep; he crouched down until it covered him up to his neck. Tossing his head back he looked at the sky, interlaced with branches; and let the cool luxury of the water lull him. After a while he moved closer to the bank and lay down on his back in the water, his head up on the bank, his feet floating. The water moved very gently around his naked flesh. This was what life was made for; such pleasures were a man's magnificence. He resolved to lie here until the water cleansed every pore and penetrated to the innermost dry centers of his bones.

A jackrabbit—he could not tell if it was the one that had led him here—popped its head out of the brush and stood uncertainly, staring at him, shaded by the massive overhang of a cottonwood limb. Charley stared back. His rifle and pistol were both up the bank with his clothes, but he made no movement toward them. Today he would not shoot anything. He let himself lie still and grinned amiably at the rabbit. Presently, assured, it moved slowly forward to the bank of the pool and stooped to test the water with its tongue. Charley studied it at close range. Presently the rabbit turned away and left. Charley closed his eyes down to slits and watched the reflected brilliance of the sky ripple along the surface of the pool when he wiggled his toes. The silence was deep and comfortable until a small flock of birds settled down in the trees and began to chirp. He shut his eyes, smiling. He did not notice when the birds flapped away.

The mud underneath was a soft mattress cradling his body. The itch that had troubled his back this morning came back to him now; he tried to scrape himself against the mud, but it was too pliable and did not scratch him sufficiently. In a moment he got up out of the water and felt the wonderful cool touch of the air against his glistening flesh. He walked barefoot to the trunk of a cottonwood and put his back to the tree, and rubbed himself up and down against it like a bear. The rough bark scratched his back satisfactorily, and still with a smile he returned to the shaded side of the pool and paddled around before again settling down on his back. He closed his eyes pleasurably and had a vision of the street of Sonora town, gray with rain, the face of the Triple Ace saloon, Gail standing in the doorway smiling. It was such a long time ago, it seemed a childhood memory. There were hard calluses on the soles of his feet and across his shoulder where the rifle-strap hung; his upper arms were thickly muscled and his legs had carried him hundreds of miles.

The water brushed him like a woman's soft hands and it occurred to him, as a surprise, that he was not lonely. It was not possible really to understand anyone; how then could any kind of real friendship be reached? Probably the truth was that humans were not comprehensible in human terms. And if you could not reach a man, you could not be his friend.

It was a crazy line of thought. His mind drifted around and his eyes, opening, followed the aimless passage of a wind-blown yellow leaf that floated near his toes. The sun had moved along above the cottonwoods, pushing the shade ahead of its rays, and he was almost into its glare. In a little while he would move. He would get up and stretch out on the bank and let the wind make him cold. He was slightly hungry. He remembered something Norval Douglas had said to him, back along the trail at a campfire. The harmonica had been making brief noises, someone tentatively breathing into it, and had stopped quickly; its owner apparently was not in a mood for it. Douglas had been chewing on a yellow stalk he had pulled out of the ground; he had been lying on one elbow, and had said in the darkness, "You can be alone for a long time, but then you want somebody to talk to. It doesn't matter very much whether he understands you, but you've got to have the illusion of getting through to him."

The floating dead leaf brushed his chin. He picked it up and crumpled it in his hand, and threw it up on the bank. That was when he heard, quite close by, the sound of a soft voice chuckling throatily.

He had to sit up in the water to look around. For a moment he almost thought it was another vision in his mind. A girl with a long graceful neck sat by his clothes. She was laughing at him; her eyes glistened. Charley stared at her. Her laughter grew more brilliant. Groping for words, Charley said, *"Buenos días."* It only increased her laughter. Charley slid into deeper water and glared at the girl. "What the hell's so funny?"

Her hand came up and pointed straight at him, and then she lay back flat on the mossy earth, lurching with laughter, soft insistent bubbling of liquid humor. Charley looked down at the surface of the water. Sunlight dappled it; ripples spread away from him. The girl was young but her body was fully molded. She wore sandals and a cheap dress. She sat up and said, "Why don't you come out of the water?" and lay back again with violent laughter. Her face was small, smooth, brown, delicate. She spoke English without hesitation, but with a strange lingering accent. She sat up again and primly smoothed the dress across her lap. Her feet came back under the dress and she sat cross-legged, her back quite slim and straight, looking at him, wiping tears from her eyes. "Very funny," Charley muttered. He wished fervently that she had left him alone in solitary possession of the grove and pool.

"You do not look like a dangerous pirate to me," the girl said.

"Who said I was a dangerous pirate?"

"You are with the party of men at the arroyo?"

"Yes."

"My father says you are pirates," she said.

"Who's your father?"

"The *alcalde*."

Charley thought of the fat man on the porch of the store, who had never stirred out of his cane-bottom chair when they had marched into Sonoyta. "Are you really a pirate?" the girl said inquisitively. "I have never seen a pirate."

"No," he said, and cursed inwardly. "I'm not a pirate."

"What are you, then?"

He hunted around for words but could find none that he felt would adequately describe him, and so he said, "I'm a traveler, that's all."

"A traveling *caballero*," the girl said musingly. A lacework of shadows from the treetops swayed slowly across her face. "Perhaps you will look more dangerous with your clothes on and a gun in your fist, eh, *caballero*?"

"You've got a fine sense of humor," Charley grumbled. "Why don't you go away?"

The girl's full lips pouted in mock anger. "The señor does not enjoy my presence."

"What would your father say?"

"My father is not here."

"Do you keep secrets from him?"

"All the time," she said cheerfully. "My father barks very

much. He does not bite." She shrugged her shoulders prettily. "He is old and lazy. What is your name?"

"Charley."

"I am Teresa."

"Pleased to meet you," he said grudgingly. He felt embarrassed, though he knew she could not see the part of him that was under water. The girl showed no sign of preparing to leave. She sat comfortably and lifted a small basket to her lap. Out of it she took a handful of berries. She ate a few of them and then looked at him out of the side of her vision. "The berries grow here," she said. "Would you like some?"

"Sure."

She held out her hand, full of berries. Charley sat where he was and tried to assume an angry glower. The girl said, "You do not have to be shy," and chuckled maddeningly. She was pretty and would have seemed out of place anywhere on the desert but here in this grove. It was all very improbable, and it would not have taken much to convince Charley that he was dreaming, except that the air on his bare shoulders was too cold and the sky too bright and the water too wet. "What do you want?" Charley said angrily.

She only looked at him out of wide, frank eyes, very dark and large. After a while she said absently, "I am staying in the house over there with my aunt. My aunt has gone to town." Then she stood up with her basket and chuckled when she looked at him, and went off through the cottonwoods with a springy gait like a young colt, long-legged and supple.

When she was gone Charley climbed out of the pool and stood restlessly on the bank. The air was cool. He lay down on his belly until he was dry. The girl's intrusion had broken up the day; for a while he resented it. But then, after he put on his clothes and buckled on his gunbelt and picked up the rifle, he looked around thoughtfully and yawned and, when he left the grove, turned uphill toward the little adobe house.

CHAPTER 17

Caborca. The church, twin-domed, dominated the town square; it sat on the east end of the plaza, backing up against a dry creekbed which, now and then, grew damp and flowed in a brown trickle; and which roared frothily during rains. Around the square stood galleried adobe structures, in part dwarfed by the tall palm trees that grew haphazardly around the town. The *padre* came out on the church steps and fingered the rope that belted his dark brown robes. A heavy woman with skin almost black, creased and cracked by weather, shuffled on her sandals, stirring up dust. The *padre* smiled and spoke a few words to her. She lifted a disreputable scarf over her head and went into the cool dimness of the church. A farmer came into the square leading his burro; on its back were packs of fresh vegetables. He led it toward the *abacería*, the grocery store. The burro was small and gray and seemed too fragile for its load; the farmer was short and bent in soiled white clothing and a wide hat. His face was out of sight in shadow. Lorenzo Rodriguez led his troops into the square at two in the afternoon, lined them up along one side of the plaza and left them standing at ease while he consulted with his officers and the leaders of the town.

It was hot. Rodriguez ran a handkerchief around his neck, under his blouse collar. He removed his hat and mopped his forehead. The two lieutenants came up and he said to the first lieutenant, "Arrange to have the men billeted in homes," and to the second lieutenant, "Commandeer enough food for our men for the next four days. Arrange for a building to be used as a mess hall." The two lieutenants saluted him and turned away. Rodriguez wiped his face with the handkerchief and turned to the city leaders—the *comisario*, the *alcalde*, the *padre*. He sighed and whipped his glance across their faces. The *alcalde* seemed to be a sensible old man. The *comisario* looked greedy. And as for the *padre*—he was a Franciscan; that was all. Rodriguez had never understood priests.

He stood young and tall, a dark man with a handsome, slightly evil face, very trim in his uniform. He held his hand over the hilt of his sword when he spoke to them. "I have been sent here by the office of Ignacio Pesquiera, who as you know has assumed the position of substitute governor since the abdication of Aguilar. My function is to inform you that there may be an attack made on this city by a group of gringo filibusters."

The *alcalde* and the *comisario* looked at one another. The *comisario* said, "Filibusters?" and his face turned fearful.

"They were invited to come here by the Gandara administration," Rodriguez said, and his voice had the sound of truth. "There will be not more than a hundred of them, I can assure you. They may heed our kind advice and turn back at Sonoyta, but that is doubtful, very doubtful. Probably they will come this way. *Por aquí*, you understand? We must be prepared for them."

The *comisario* swallowed and said, "How long do we have?"

Rodriguez shrugged. "Perhaps two days, perhaps two weeks."

"How shall we prepare for them?"

"I will take it upon myself to train and equip the young men of the town," Rodriguez said. "You will have all the young men report to my sergeants for training. They will be issued muskets and ammunition. As for the rest, the women and old men and children, I suggest you organize them into groups, encourage them to stay under cover away from the center of town, and keep with them enough provisions to withstand a brief siege if it becomes necessary."

"A siege?"

"I hope that will not occur," Rodriguez said. "Already I have posted guards some distance up the roads. If the filibusters come, we should be given ample warning of their approach. I hope to meet them outside the town and bring an end to it. But they are better armed than we are—one has to do the best he can with what he has, you see. It may be necessary for us to draw them into the town so that we can hold them here until General Gabilondo arrives with reinforcements."

"*Por Diós*," the *padre* muttered. "We must pray for our people."

"You might say a prayer or two for the filibusters too," Rodriguez said with a small grin.

"Bah," the *padre* said, and spat. "They are pigs. But if they walk on two legs I suppose they are entitled to God's mercy."

"You are most charitable, good priest."

The *padre* turned toward the church, his robes flapping. Rodriguez said to the *comisario*, "I am afraid the town stores will have to be made available to my men. We do not wish to tax the town more than necessary, but my men must eat."

"Of course," the *comisario* said reluctantly.

"Do not be so sad," Rodriguez murmured drily. "I only seek to save your town, *comisario*."

"Or perhaps use it for a battleground," the *comisario* replied. "Which is it, Captain?"

"Do you want me to take my troops with me and leave?" Rodriguez demanded immediately. "I should like to see what might happen to this town of yours if the filibusters were given free rein to sack it."

The glum *comisario* spread his hands. "All right," he said. "All right. You will have our cooperation, Captain. It is just that no man wishes to see his home turned into a barracks."

"Of course. I understand perfectly," Rodriguez said coolly. "My tongue is dry, gentlemen. Is there a cantina where we might continue our talk?"

"This way," the *alcalde* said.

Inside the cantina it was cool and dark. The barkeep drew three *cervezas* and set the mugs before them. Rodriguez took his beer back to a rickety hand-hewn table in a corner of the room where it seemed coolest, and sat, adjusting his sword so that it did not dig against his ribs. Not far away a girl sat listlessly over a glass of tequila, staring without interest at the face of the fat young man with her. The girl wore a low-scoop blouse and a flower in her hair. Probably the local *puta*, Rodriguez thought, but she was less ugly than most of her kind. Her eyes flicked past him, hesitated, and came back. Rodriguez dipped his head to her and the girl smiled. That would do very nicely for later, Rodriguez decided, and thought for a moment of his wife in Hermosillo. He said to the *alcalde*, "It might be a good idea if you were to call a meeting of the townspeople and let me explain to them what we are doing here."

"Yes," the *alcalde* said. "I had thought the same thing."

"Perhaps," said the *comisario*, "perhaps we should not alarm the people unduly."

"They must be told," Rodriguez said, disliking the man for his obtuseness. "Would you rather have them wonder what we are doing here and resent the billeting of my troops in their houses? They must be prepared, and it is best that they know what is going on as soon as possible. As it is, enough of them will run away."

"Very well," the *comisario* grumbled.

The *alcalde* said, "I will have someone ring the church bell," and got up from his beer to pick a path through the tables and go out into the sun.

The *comisario* was frugal enough to finish his beer before he went. Rodriguez was happy to see him leave. Afterward he sat and smiled at the girl with the flower in her hair. He remembered when he had first met his wife. She had been a girl then, no older than this whore, but she had carried herself with a fine composure. It had been, he remembered, at a ball given by the prefect of Hermosillo. A very fine ball. Chandeliers and wine, fine ladies and music. And from that he had come away to this dusty little town on the Rio Concepcion to fight against an army of foreigners. He drank his beer down and touched the hilt of his sword. At Ures they thought him a dandy, a wealthy young man who liked to show himself off in a uniform. He would demonstrate to them that he was as good a fighting soldier as any of them. He smiled at the girl with the flower in her hair.

*   *   *

When Charley returned to camp in the evening it was time to eat. He spoke to no one, ate a lonely meal, and afterward cleaned his utensils with sand. The sun went down and the harmonica

146

breathed its sorrowful way across the camp; men settled down to play cards, soap saddles, talk, sleep. There was an attitude of confidence in the faces roundabout. Charley felt adrift. He went back over the long afternoon's conversation with the girl. Flirting and small talk—arts at which he was not expert. He had spoken, though, of little things: of the cool pleasure of the shaded cottonwood pool, of the plans in his mind, hanging there vaguely, to build a little house in Mexico and work the ground for gold, of things he had seen in Stockton and Sacramento and San Francisco, of childhood recollections of New Orleans—cotton barkers hawking at an auction, the filthy old streets, darkies hauling river barges with thick ropes bent around their shoulders, dandy swells in their finery stalking the walks, his stepfather sending him to a corner saloon with a pail for beer. The girl had showed wistful interest, and in her turn had told of a dusty little horned-toad she had kept as a pet, of a time when her father the *alcalde* had whipped a youth because the youth had spoken to her, of the little things that touched her heart. Hers was a romantic soul and she spoke of such things as birdsongs and a long ago friendship with a coyote cub. It was all very strange and in a way sad, for it made him think of other places and he began to wish he had not come along on this senseless journey.

When the sky was star-peppered and campfires blossomed red and men settled in, Charley got up softly from his blankets and walked out into the desert alone. The night air carried the sharp, raw scent of the wild country. Fine short wrinkles converged around his eyes when he looked up toward the faint glitter of distant stars. Dry branches rustled before small winds.

Indecision plagued him; he wondered if he had made a mistake coming here; he was afraid. Always inclined to stuff his feelings down inside where they wouldn't show, he walked slowly and listened to the crunch of his feet and the occasional crackle of a creosote twig or cholla segment that would break underfoot in the dark, and in spite of his aloneness in the world his expression displayed none of the tugging that went on in his soul. He wished he could know, for certain, whether to quit or go on—or whether it made any real difference whatever he did. In that mood, a sudden mood, he sat down on his haunches and tossed pebbles.

He had come to know that no one ever had much warning of the conflicts brought by each moment's waking; there had to be times when, taken by surprise, he had to act and stand behind that act forever, even though he might have acted for no reason whatever. He had the feeling that most of his life had resulted not so much from will as from accident. If that were not true, there was no adequate reason for his being here.

And the end result of it was that no living person had a claim on him and he had no claim on anybody. It made him recall what Norval Douglas had said to him one day—that every man had to live by himself, for himself; that was as it should be. "When you've got no one to please but yourself," Douglas had told him, "then you're all right. It's a mistake to begin thinking you matter to somebody."

He didn't know. A coyote yapped across the night from some distant point. He got up and went back, slipped into camp without bothering anyone, and rolled up in his blanket, thinking of the girl with the long neck on the mossy bank of the water hole. It was some time before he got to sleep.

CHAPTER 18

Sus came up from the camp and stood before Crabb, and looked at his feet. Crabb said, "Well?"

"Well, what?"

"We're ready to leave," Crabb said, looking forward at the men lined up, the pack animals grouped together, the officers mounted on chafing horses. Crabb stood by the head of his horse, ready to mount. "McKinney should be along any time now with the wounded. You'll give him my instructions?"

"I will," Sus said, with a tone of stiffness.

Crabb took the attitude of a man letting pent-up air out of his lungs. "Good. I was half-expecting an argument."

"Would it have done any good?"

"No."

Sus smiled vaguely. Crabb came forward leading the horse, his hand outstretched. Sus took it gravely. Afterward Crabb swung up into the saddle, a trifle awkwardly; he was no horseman. Sus stood back and touched his hatbrim. Crabb wheeled away from him and cantered to the head of the column. Sus watched them go, sixty-eight men, including the tall distant shape of Norval Douglas on the horizon, waving them forward into Mexico. Sus wondered when he would see them again.

He stood by the arroyo until the last of the long gray worm of men had crawled out of sight over the distant gentle slope. By then the sun was high enough to warm the earth and make it glitter. He looked over the abandoned campground—the dead signs of campfires, the horse-hollow grazed bare, the confusion of footprints and litter of discarded small articles that marked a camp and said, They passed by here. *Pasaron por aquí.* Perhaps one day someone would put up a monument commemorating their passage.

The dust had all settled; the land was still. Sus looked back on the months behind them and found himself most surprised by one thing: that the trek had not been marked by the kind of easy comradeship that should have been part of it. It was not as if he stood here left behind by a company of friends. He could remember a decade ago when his father had come back from the war, which had really not been much of a war, for California's independence. On a field above the town they had mustered out the troops, and afterward there had been laughing and pushing, men with arms about each other's shoulders, hats thrown in the air, guns wildly discharged. His father had brought home three comrades, fed them and given them shelter. But this expedition had none of that feeling; and he knew now that he had discovered its fault. There were too many resentments, suspicions, fears among these men. He had not recognized it when he had walked among them, but he saw it now in the ashes of the abandoned fires. Intrigues and secret conflicts were the premises here. There was no real common goal. In spite of the artificial bolstering that Crabb's inspiring oratory had given them, there was no strong loyalty in the group. Crabb had been right about them. Private ambitions and greed drove most of the men. Some of them, like McCoun, were full of bluster but at bottom afraid.

It was not an encouraging line of thought. He turned slowly toward Sonoyta and began to walk that way.

By the time he reached the plaza he was hungry. In Redondo's store he ate some cheese and tortillas, spiced with chili peppers and washed down with dark beer. When he went back outside, Redondo was in his customary position on the porch, one boot cocked up on the rail, picking his teeth. Redondo said in Spanish, "Your friends have all departed."

"Yes."

"Why do you remain?"

"There are more men coming along. I am to meet them here."

"More men?" Redondo said musingly, and shrugged absently, as if in the long run it made no difference.

"Some of them may be too ill to travel farther," Sus said. "I am to take care of them. Where can they be billeted?"

"Not here," Redondo said promptly.

"Why not here?"

"No one would take them in," Redondo said in an offhand way.

"Why?"

"The people of this town know what you are. They do not wish to be caught harboring filibusters."

Sus made a scoffing noise. "These men are sick. They will harm no one."

"That is what we intend to make sure of. You might put them up at Dunbar's trading post. That is a few miles north and east of here. It is not in Mexico."

"Are we in Mexico here?"

"In truth," said the thickset *alcalde*, "it is a matter of opinion. The opinion at Ures is that we are in Mexico. Governor Aguilar will probably have troops here soon enough."

"What for?"

Redondo made no answer. He studied the damp softened tip of his toothpick. After a moment he threw it away and found another in his pocket. Sus wondered darkly if Redondo was bluffing, but decided there would be little point in that. But what did it mean? He could not make sense out of Pesquiera's sending troops here to Sonoyta. It would be locking the barn after the theft of the horse. He said, "How far is Dunbar's trading post, *Alcalde?*"

"Not far. An hour's ride, perhaps less."

"Dunbar is a *Norteamericano?*"

"He is Scottish, I think."

"Perhaps we will go there, then."

"It would be wise for you to go there."

"*Gracias,*" Sus said drily.

"*De nada.*" The fat man twisted his neck around to look at the thermometer. "In the shade," he muttered, "ninety-four degrees." He made a clucking noise with his tongue. "It is not yet April. What will July be like?"

"Worse."

"I am sure of that," said Redondo.

Sus went inside the store and scooped a handful of salt crackers from the open barrel. The afternoon proceeded to drag by. He was to find that it would be two more days before McKinney arrived; during that time Sus amused himself as best he could. The next night he drank alone, and on the second morning he went for a walk in the desert, kicking stones, until it became hot and he returned after a splash in the pool to Redondo's shaded porch. Redondo sat in his usual place; once in a while they exchanged comments. Customers drifted in and out of the place; it must have been Saturday, for a good number of farmers were in town from outlying areas. How they found it possible to grow crops in this country was beyond Sus, but he guessed there must be occasional green canyons in the roundabout hills.

About noon a young, lean rider trotted into the square and stepped down at the well to drink and water his horse, and then came dragging his musical spurs to the store, and said to Redondo, "I wish to speak to you." After a look at Sus the young man added, "Privately, *por favor*."

Redondo conferred with the man inside the store, and afterward, when the young man went off to the stable, Redondo said to Sus, "The troops are coming. I hope your men arrive soon, amigo."

"How soon will the troops come?"

"Tomorrow, probably in the morning."

"I see." Sus frowned toward the northwestern desert, from which McKinney must come.

Through the afternoon he began to chafe. Then, at about four o'clock, a rising column of dust to the northwest brought him to his feet. He stood at the edge of the porch, rocking on the balls of his feet, and said to Redondo, "Point out to me the way to Dunbar's store."

Redondo did not rise. He flung out an arm. "Northeast. You go through that notch between the two round hills. It is one mile beyond that. You will see it from the hills. It is surrounded by trees; there is a spring."

"Thanks," Sus said, and stepped off the porch. He walked across the plaza and out of town, going toward the advancing dust cloud. Hot air met him in the face and sultry heat lay close along the ground.

Distances were deceiving along the desert flats. He had walked almost five miles before he was able to separate the men and horses from the dust cloud. He sat down in the near-worthless shadow of a stunted paloverde to wait for them. It took almost an hour; presently he recognized McKinney, and stood up to wave his arm in signal.

McKinney drew rein, halting the column. Sus looked back along the ranks. Four men clung to saddles; the rest, fifteen in number, walked, some of them leading pack animals. McKinney greeted Sus without enthusiasm. Dust caked his dry flesh and his eyes were bloodshot. He climbed wearily off the saddle and said, "How far is it to Sonoyta?"

"A few miles. But I've got instructions for you."

"Go ahead," McKinney said. He seemed washed out.

"The Mexicans are making threats against us," Sus told him. "The general decided to go on to the Concepcion and meet Cosby there before Pesquiera makes up his mind to act against us."

McKinney looked very tired. He nodded. "I see." He looked back along the line of men, expectantly waiting. "How long ago did he leave?"

"Two days ago. They were making good time."

"At the rate we're traveling," McKinney said, "it will take a week to catch them."

"How many men do you have who aren't fit to go on?"

McKinney made a gesture with his thumb. "The four on horseback." He removed his hat and rubbed his bald, pointed head. Sus looked at the four men. They all hung precariously to their saddles.

Sus drew in a long breath and said quietly, "Your instructions are to follow the general and catch up as quickly as you can. I'll take these four men with me to Dunbar's trading post."

"All right," McKinney said, showing no surprise. He added absently, "I wonder what happened to the men who went to Tucson for reinforcements."

"They haven't had time to get here yet."

"I guess not." McKinney looked back down the line. "We'll camp here. I'll send somebody in to Sonoyta for water and supplies."

"They'll find the pickings poor."

McKinney shrugged. He didn't seem to care. Sus said, "If I were you I'd try to be out of here by morning. Some Mexican troops will be coming here sometime tomorrow."

"Fine," McKinney said, "fine and dandy. Do you want to take those four with you now?"

"All right," Sus said.

*   *   *

In the night, Sus thought he heard gunshots faint in the distance, but he was not sure. It might be a trick of the night winds of the desert. Just the same, he quickened his steps.

In the past fortnight he had watched carefully over the four men at the trading post. Two of them were so ill they were unable to sit up to eat. He had hired two fat Sonoyta women to care for them, and he had brought corn-flour tortillas, eggs, and milk from town for them. But on the second day the troops had come, and the villagers had become afraid. On the fifth day all of them closed their doors to him and no woman would come to Dunbar's to help care for the sick. Redondo remained noncommittal, but said the soldiers would keep to their side of the border. Rumors of battles and massacres came up from the Concepcion valley on the lips of Indians and traveling men; it all sounded unreasonable.

Sus walked across the pale desert on legs that had grown muscular. He carried five precious eggs, stolen. He traveled through the hill notch and saw a lamp burning at Dunbar's; all seemed well. Then horsemen drummed forward in the darkness, a large party, and he knew it was too late to seek concealment; they had seen him silhouetted. He stood still, waiting for them to come up.

The horsemen were shouting: "*Viva México! Mueran los gringos!*" Death to the gringos. What did it mean?

A hoarse voice shot forward from the horsemen: "Sus—Sus Ainsa."

"*Sí,*" he answered warily. He touched his gun but saw immediately the patent uselessness of that gesture. The riders were all around him. The man who had spoken dismounted and bounded forward, cuffing back his hat. "Sus—you remember me?"

"Jesús Ojeda," he said, and smiled uncertainly. "*Como está?*"

"*Bien,*" Ojeda said, and clasped his shoulders. Then the grin went away from his cheeks and he said, "I must arrest you, my friend."

"What?"

"I am ordered to arrest you."

"What for?"

"I do not know."

"You can't," Sus said. "This is not Mexican soil."

Ojeda shook his head gravely. "I have my orders, amigo. I must obey."

"But you can't!" Sus found that he was shouting. He resolved to quiet down. He looked up at the others and then realized that they were coming not from the direction of Mexico, but from the trading post. Reluctant understanding seeped into his mind and he said slowly, "Jesús—Jesús, old friend, what have you done to my friends down there?" And held his breath.

Ojeda turned his palms up. "They are dead."

"All of them?"

"All dead, all four."

Fury bunched Sus's fists. "What in God's name for?"

Ojeda's reaction was the same shrug, the same palms turned up. "I told you, amigo—I am under orders. I am a soldier."

"Those men were sick."

"All right," Ojeda said mildly. "Now they are sick no more."

"God," Sus breathed. "What has turned you into a butcher, Jesús?"

Ojeda said nothing in reply. He stepped forward to lift the gun from Sus's holster, and rammed it into his own belt. "We will go now."

"Where?"

"To Mexico," Ojeda said.

CHAPTER 19

Two weeks before the arrest of Sus Ainsa, the column of seventy with Crabb at its head entered the valley of the Rio Concepcion. It was a hot morning, the sky was blue and clear, dust raveled above the column, and Crabb had thrown out guards on either flank to watch the horizons. At the same time in various places a number of incidents took place. At Ures, Acting Governor Pesquiera visited former Governor Aguilar's cell, spoke desultorily to the man, and went back to his office to pace the floor, restively awaiting news from his far-flung outposts. Gabilondo was at El Claro on the Rio de San Ignacio, raising an army in a leisurely way. Giron, also recruiting, was to join Gabilondo later in the week at Pitiquito, where the San Ignacio had its confluence with the Concepcion, not far upstream from Caborca. In San Francisco, fifteen hundred miles away, a prostitute whose name was unknown stopped at the cemetery to put flowers on General Cosby's grave. At San Perfecto, not too far south of Sonoyta on the way to the Concepcion valley, Captain Freeman McKinney was giving his weary men a day's rest in the shade. In Caborca, Captain Lorenzo Rodriguez received from his scouts intelligence of the advance of the party of filibusters toward the town. He acted accordingly. At Sonoyta, on the border, Redondo was sitting on his porch picking his teeth and Sus was down at the pool bathing. At Tucson, Arizona, about two hundred miles northeast of Caborca as the crow might fly, the men who had left Crabb's group at Yuma—Charles Tozer and Bob Wood—had organized a relief party that included such prominent Arizona pioneers as John G. Capron and Granville H. Oury. By now this party, going to the aid of Crabb, numbering twenty-six men, had left Tucson and was in the vicinity of Calabasas. And twenty-five hundred miles east by northeast, the populace was deep in consideration of the recent inaugural address of President James Buchanan and the Supreme Court's decision in the case of one Dred Scott, a Negro slave who had sued for his freedom on the grounds that he resided in a free-soil territory; the Court refused Scott's appeal and held that he was not a citizen of the United States and thus was not entitled to sue in a Federal court. In New York, John Butterfield was busy organizing a transcontinental stagecoach line to be known as the Butterfield Overland Mail. In San Francisco, Filomena Ainsa Crabb reread for the eleventh time the last letter she had received from her husband. It had been written at Fort Yuma. At Sonora, California, a small fire began in the back of the Triple Ace saloon but was brought under control before it did much damage.

*   *   *

Lorenzo Rodriguez sat in the dim corner of the cantina and admired the whore who sat at the table with him, a flower in her hair. The *alcalde* came in and went immediately to Rodriguez's table and, ignoring the woman, said, "I have organized the noncombatants in their houses with provisions."

"Good," Rodriguez said. The *alcalde* stood hesitantly until Rodriguez waved his hand. "You had better get to a safe place, amigo. The filibusters are not far from town."

"Then why do you sit here?"

"It does not pay to hurry," Rodriguez said mildly. "They will be along presently. My scouts keep me informed. Go, now."

The *alcalde* said, "Is there nothing else I can do? I used to be a good shot."

"Post yourself on the square, then, with a musket."

"I will." The *alcalde* left. Rodriguez met the *puta's* yellow-toothed smile and touched the flower in her hair. He was thinking of his wife in Hermosillo and wondering with what wealthy *don* she had slept the night past. He thought of his genteel life there and of the sordid dimness of this little cantina, smelling of stale beer and tequila and mescal and tobacco smoke, but mostly of beer. He said, "Marguerita."

"*Sí, patrón?*"

"I hope we are able to defeat the filibusters promptly. It would be unfortunate if Gabilondo arrived in time to take over. I want the credit for this victory to myself. It will make them look up to me in Hermosillo and in Ures. I will earn a promotion. No longer will they think of me as a young playboy using the sword as his toy. I do not play at being a soldier, Marguerita."

"No."

"I am a good soldier. I shall prove it to them."

"Of course," she said. He ignored the brittle calculated quality of her smile.

The *comisario* came in wheezing. "Is it true? Are they advancing on us, the filibusters?"

"Of course it is true," Rodriguez said, looking on the man with cool contempt.

The *comisario* looked flabbergasted. "And yet you sit here sipping beer and entertaining this whore?"

"She needs no entertainment," Rodriguez said imperturbably. "On the contrary, good *comisario*, she entertains me, you see." He smiled.

"Fool," shouted the *comisario*. "Do something!"

"What would you have me do?"

The *comisario* pounded his fist into his palm. His cheeks seemed about to explode. It was quite comical, Rodriguez thought. The *comisario* was just like an actor out of the opera at Hermosillo, playing a comic part. Rodriguez slipped his fingers along the soft round heaviness of the woman's arm and said, "Perhaps you would have me go out on the plaza and make great speeches to my men, telling them how it is their patriotic duty to fight and die for their country. Is that it, *comisario*?"

The *comisario* seemed to be purpling. Rodriguez chuckled. "Calm yourself," he said. "Go home and lock your door."

The *comisario* looked away and wrung his hands and slowly shuffled away. Rodriguez laughed. He squeezed the *puta's* arm and drank the last of his beer and said to her, "I shall return presently, Marguerita," and left the cantina.

Sunlight made him squint. Lieutenant Corella, who was a stocky man from the mines of the Arizpe district and currently Rodriguez's second-in-command, trotted across the square on his horse and saluted lazily. "They are still six miles out," he said. "There is no cover out there to surround them from. When they come a couple of miles closer, perhaps we can set up an ambuscade in the thickets."

"I will think on it," Rodriguez said. "Put your horse up. Whatever we do, it will be an infantry operation. We haven't enough horses to mount the men."

Corella saluted again and went away. Rodriguez looked around. All seemed satisfactory. Armed men were posted all along the plaza—in doorways, in windows, on roofs, at corners. Rodriguez smiled, knowing that his smile of confidence would give them heart. Throwing his chest out, he took a deep breath and patted the revolver at his side. He decided to set up an ambush where the road came up to the outskirts of town, between two wheat fields.

*   *   *

During the brief rest halt, Crabb spoke to the men. Charley sat on a rock and listened. Crabb was talking of the provisions to be had in Caborca and of the prospects of soon meeting up with General Cosby's army somewhere on the river below. The men listened with polite interest. The fiery spirit that had blazed in them on the night of Crabb's speech at Sonoyta was reduced by now to an ill-fed flicker; once again they were footsore and weary and resentful of the unfriendly treatment they had been accorded at the hands of the few Mexicans they had met along the way. Charley sensed a feeling of uncertainty that grew and growled among the men. They were here now; this was the promised land. But threats of violence lay around them in the barren open stretches of the land and in the uncompromising hatred they met everywhere in the faces of Mexican people. Gringo travelers had instilled in them that hostility; it had not been uncommon for Americans, traveling through this country on their way west, to raid farms, rape daughters, steal, and burn.

All around, at varying distances, lifted round ridges and barren mountains. Vegetation here was only slightly more rich than it had been in the border country to the north. Creosote remained the principal ground-cover; the soil was still tan and powdery. But ahead of them to the left of a low hill was a dense pattern of dark green that marked the irrigated fields and treetops of Caborca town. Yucca stalks, maguey, ocotillo, manzanita—the various shrubs and strange cacti of the desert dotted everything in sight. Lizards and gophers were plentiful, the latter chiefly evident by the holes they left treacherously in the ground.

John Edmonson said, when Crabb had finished his speechmaking, "I'd hoped for more than this."

Charley nodded his agreement. It seemed a spare, poor place after all the promises they had heard. "This isn't the mining country," Charley said. "The mines are up in the mountains, I hear, where there's a lot of timber."

"Timber," Edmonson said. "I'd like to see that. I wonder how far it is?"

Norval Douglas came trotting back from his advance position and stepped down to confer with Crabb. Then McCoun gave the order to form up, and they began to march forward. Douglas rode with Crabb and McCoun. Presently they came upon a dusty rutted road and turned toward town. The sun seemed particularly savage. In front of Charley walked Samuel Kimmel and Bill Randolph. Jim Woods was behind Charley and now and then Charley could hear the ex-saloonkeeper's caustic commentary on the country they passed through. "Give me hell," Woods said drily. Up front on horseback, Captain McDowell's beard showed livid red when he turned to look back. Walls of palm trees closed down on the road and then, ahead, the trees stopped and the road traveled between two fields high with uncut wheat. Beyond that were the first buildings of the town's edge. Walking down this path between the orderly rows of palms, Charley was reminded of boyhood and shady lanes among the willows in the bayou country.

The front of the column left the palm-bordered area and moved up between the wheat fields, and in that instant a man in uniform stepped out of the wheat into the leaders' path and held up his hand. The man carried a carbine in his fist.

The column halted. Charley stood looking ahead with curiosity, craning his neck to look around Bill Randolph's big shape. The Mexican was talking insistently, gesturing emphatically with his hands. Crabb was shaking his head. Norval Douglas was with them, apparently translating back and forth from English to Spanish. The Mexican waved threateningly with his rifle; in answer, Crabb drew his revolver and pointed it at the Mexican. Charley heard Edmonson voicing what was in everyone's mind: "I wonder what the devil they're talking about."

"Looks like a Mex officer to me," someone said.

"Maybe they're afraid we're going to loot the town or something."

"That might not be too bad an idea," Jim Woods said. "I've had just about enough of their sneers."

At that moment the Mexican drew back, evidently rebuffed by something Crabb had said; his back stiff, the Mexican turned toward the silent wheat fields and shouted what sounded like a command.

The sound of a single gunshot cut off the Mexican's shout directly in its middle. The Mexican collapsed on the ground. Crabb was standing over him; Crabb's gun was smoking. Charley stared at the form of the Mexican, crumpled and small in the road. "Holy Jesus," someone muttered in an awed tone of voice. "What the hell did he do that for?"

Then gunfire erupted from the wheat fields.

Up front, men wheeled and broke in confusion. Charley saw Crabb running back toward the palms, McCoun at his heels. For a brief span of time, Norval Douglas and Captain McDowell held their ground, firing revolvers into the swaying stalks of wheat; then they too whirled back toward the protection of the thick-trunked palms. Stunned men stood frozen by the abruptness of it. Muzzle flashes bloomed from the wheat fields; as if from a distance, Charley heard the boom of musket shots. All around him men swung in turmoil. He snapped his jaw shut and made an awkward dive toward the side of the road, and rolled behind the cover of a tree trunk. The dive took the wind out of him. When he caught his breath he looked around him and saw that no one remained on the road.

A swarm of men issued from the wheat fields on both sides of the road and ran forward shooting. In the confusion Charley was mainly aware of the rising stink of powdersmoke and the wild shouts of men and the improbable loudness of the massed gunfire. Then he realized that men all about him were shooting back. He groped for the rifle, swung it off his shoulder and yanked the big hammer back to full cock. He pointed it into the approaching mass of arms and legs and guns, and pulled the trigger.

It was inhumanly stupid, the way the Mexicans advanced in a tight-packed body along the twin ruts of the road. "Stupid—stupid—stupid," the words kept echoing in his mind and he realized he was shouting aloud. Men to either side of him had

161

settled down coolly, picking targets. Charley fumbled with the ramrod and then flung it down in disgust, picking up his revolver and firing six shots at the Mexicans, each shot on the heels of the last. He heard men cursing at the tops of their voices. Mexicans were dropping in unbelievable numbers; and in a very short time the cluster of men broke, weaved, and tumbled back. Stupidly, they did not get out of the road; they ran straight down the ruts. A few of them dived aside into the concealment of the wheat fields, but until they ran beyond rifle range there was a mass of targets for the gringos' percussion guns.

A sudden stillness settled down. Something was hissing in his ears—the ringing aftermath of gunfire. The town ahead was quiet. The body of the Mexican officer lay not far away where Crabb had shot him; beyond that on the road were the sprawled corpses of men. One of them was crawling very slowly toward the wheat fields. Charley saw Bill Randolph lift his gun and shoot that man. After that there were no more shots. The bodies in the road were riddled with bullets. Charley looked around and saw no dead men among the Americans; he did not even see any wounds.

Someone said, "My God—My God." It was old John Edmonson, lying behind a palm. His gun had not been fired.

Acrid sulphur fumes filled Charley's nostrils. Mechanically, because he saw others doing it, he reloaded his rifle and revolver. There was the sound of retching somewhere behind him. He did not turn to look. Ahead, General Crabb stepped out into the road and lifted both arms over his head. "Gather round me," he shouted.

Men crawled out of the ditches and out from behind trees and walked warily down the road, eyes and guns trained on the wheat fields. Nothing stirred there; it was evident the Mexicans had broken and retreated to town. Charley got up and found his legs unsteady. He took an uncertain step forward and saw Edmonson still lying behind the tree, not moving, staring at the earth under his face. Charley walked to him and stooped. "Are you hurt?"

"What?"

162

"Are you hurt?"

"I don't think so." Edmonson checked himself over. Then he shook his head. His face had a numb, dull look. "No," he said. "I'm all right."

"Come on, then." Charley took his arm and helped him get up. Edmonson shook his head as if to clear it. Charley said, "Pick up your rifle."

"My rifle." Edmonson stood dumbly. Charley reached down and gathered up the gun and handed it to Edmonson, who looked at it. Presently he slung it over his shoulder and presented a shaking smile. "Come on," Charley said, and led him forward.

Men stood around in tight ranks, all of them listening to Crabb. "They attacked us without warning," Crabb was saying. "We have the right to carry the fight to them, and by God we will. I intend to take this town. Does anyone object?"

Very possibly, Charley thought, it was Crabb's shortest speech. He put down the impulse to giggle. A muttering roar like something from an animal's throat grew in the crowd. Charley felt weak in the ankles. They began to move forward, spreading out along the sides of the road. McDowell and Holliday came back giving orders to the horse-holders. McDowell looked like a Biblical prophet; the long jaw of his red beard moved energetically when he talked. He said, "Keep to cover and watch for snipers," and, "Keep those horses in the rear." Holliday was drawling in a more relaxed way: "Keep your Goddamn guns loaded." Keep this and keep that—Charley moved in a daze of confusion. Up the road beyond the wheat fields he could see the walls of small farm plots that bordered the road. Men seemed to be dodging around behind those walls. All the officers' horses went to the rear and men moved forward on the edges of the road until a sporadic musketry began from the adobe walls and the officers got down on one knee to return the fire. Charley had a clear picture of Norval Douglas calmly firing his revolver at slow intervals toward the walls that closed down on the road ahead. It was all very impersonal; targets were seldom visible and did not seem to relate to humanity. Shadow-figures, seen only briefly, fell back from the walls and he saw Crabb marching briskly forward down the road, followed by the officers. The column picked up speed and Charley found himself walking at a good pace, as if they were out alone in the desert marching toward a water hole.

The column halted between the adobe walls. Several men vaulted over them and there were a few gunshots. Then the officers came down the line singling out men. McDowell stopped in front of Charley and said, "You handled that gun well back there, Evans," and Charley wondered when the captain had got time to notice. McDowell said, "You'll go with me around to the left. We'll cut through town around from the east side and meet the others on the square. You too, Randolph."

After that, in company with half a dozen others, Charley followed the red-bearded captain past the end of the adobe wall and, cautiously, around a building corner. They skirted the edge of town, making a quarter-circle around it, and met no resistance, though Charley kept his rifle cocked and jumped several times when he saw what appeared to be movements in the shadows. They passed slot-windowed adobes one by one; each time McDowell would kick the door open and lunge inside, and each time the building would prove to be empty. McDowell said, "They were ready for us. They're all probably forted up in the middle of town."

Charley swept the rooftops and inspected shadows until his eyes began to ache. A slight tremor had invaded his hands and he was afraid that even if he did shoot at something, he would probably miss. He kept having the vision of the crowd of Mexicans coming down the road to avenge their gunshot leader—a mass of bodies and eyes, arms and legs into which he had poured his ammunition. He did not know whether he had hit anyone, but had the feeling he must have. It was strange, he thought, that he felt no particular reaction—unless he were to count the trembling.

"Look out, now," McDowell said. They were slipping along the side wall of a 'dobe. McDowell flattened himself against the end of the wall and poked his head around for a look down the street. Then he gestured with his free hand and went around out of sight.

Bill Randolph followed him; Charley was right behind Bill. The three of them stopped at the head of the street. From here they could see part of the plaza, two blocks distant. The twin domes of the church lifted above the rooftops of squat yellow-gray buildings. Bill's tongue came out and moistened his lips. His head was defiantly set back on his thick Prussian neck. The three other men came around the corner and stood with them. The street appeared deserted—dry, sunlit, dusty. Quite crisp and loud was the sound of Bill's rifle-hammer drawing back to full cock. There was sweat on Charley's palms and he rubbed them, one at a time, against the coarse grain of his trousers. His hat felt tight and he pushed it back an inch. From some other part of town came the rapid chatter of gunfire. It lasted only a short while. "Come on," McDowell said. "Stay close to the buildings."

Bill Randolph and two of the others trotted across the head of the street and started down the opposite side. Charley got up on the sidewalk behind McDowell. They walked forward putting one boot in front of the other. Once Charley thought he saw a man's hatbrim outlined above a roof across the street, but when he turned it was gone. A few more shots went off in another part of town. He wondered where everyone had gone. Had they deserted the town in the face of the gringo riflemen? It didn't seem likely.

A Mexican in a wide sombrero with crossed belts running from shoulder to waist came in a rush from a doorway a block down the street, shouting in Spanish. He had a musket and he lifted it. Charley thought it was aimed right at him. He tried to bring his gun around, but it swung with ponderous slowness. A single shot crashed against his ears and the Mexican spun half-around, dropped his gun, and wheeled back into the doorway from which he had come. McDowell stopped to reload his rifle. "We'll have to go in after that one," he said. "He'll probably have a knife."

But then the Mexican leaped out of the doorway again. Somewhere he had armed himself with a huge flintlock horse pistol, over which he leaned. It was a strange sight—the man standing in the middle of the street bent over a pistol, trying to get it cocked. Charley heard a roar of laughter and saw Bill Randolph take a casual aim and shoot. The Mexican's feet slipped out from under him and he fell in an ungainly sprawl. The pistol flipped away from him. He raised his head and stared at it. Standing where he was, Bill Randolph calmly reloaded and took aim again, but then the Mexican's face turned and dropped into the dirt, and Bill did not fire. "Jesus Christ," Charley heard McDowell mutter. "What a Goddamn mess." They went foot by foot downstreet toward the edge of the plaza. At every window they stopped to reconnoiter; at every door they stopped and pushed inside, guns ready. Every place seemed deserted. Furniture stood empty. In a window across the street, behind Bill and his men, a Mexican appeared with a shotgun. Charley's breath hung up in his chest. The shotgun muzzle lifted and Charley turned his gun on that man and fired. He had not aimed his shot; he had only pointed and pulled the trigger. But the Mexican sagged across the sill and dropped his shotgun. Charley swallowed. The Mexican did not move at all. Still, he was far enough away to remain an impersonal target. Charley had yet to see death close up.

"Reload," McDowell told him, and went on down the street.

CHAPTER 20

"God damn it," said Jim Woods, "I knew there was something crazy. It's April Fool's Day!"

A rattle of laughter went around the big room. Crabb's voice cut across it sharply: "Watch your posts."

Men crouched with their rifles laid across windowsills. The massive front door was barred with a heavy timber. In a back bedroom two wounded men lay on luxurious beds. Furniture had been pushed aside in the big parlor; supplies were stacked in the center of the room. Periodically a shot came from the church across the square where the Mexican troops had fortified themselves. In the front windows, Bill Randolph and Norval Douglas and five other men answered the fire. The smell and taste of powdersmoke was powerful and bitter. Charley sat in a front corner pressing the bandage that covered a bullet-burn on his left arm. Around him men cursed and fretted. He felt detached and cool and slightly lightheaded. The events of the last hour were a blur in his mind—battling armies surging back and forth across the square; a line of men driving the Mexicans into the walls of the church while behind them another line of men feverishly unloaded the pack animals and rushed the supplies into this thick-walled mansion opposite the church. He had only a vague idea of what had happened; he did not understand how they had achieved the sanctuary of this fortress-like house and in the doing of it only suffered two minor casualties and a few bullet scratches like his own. Across the room a small group of men was laughing and spraying obscenities, talking contemptuously of Mexican marksmanship. The Mexicans had been scared; but Charley did not laugh at them. He knew how they felt. He remembered the women, the children, the old men spilling back from invaded homes, driven back from all sides and trapped in the open plaza, fired at from the streets and falling back into the convent beside the old church. Horses rearing and screaming. Men cutting the packsaddle cinches and dragging the loaded saddles back into the big house. A line of men crouched down and squinting across their sights. The Mexican troops, confused and leaderless, backing into the church. A stocky Mexican officer who looked more like a miner than a soldier, finally taking charge and laying siege to the Americans who had gathered in this great sprawling house which must have belonged to the wealthiest citizen of Caborca.

Old John Edmonson came over and stooped over him, looming in the strange shadows. "Do you want a drink?"

"Yes."

Edmonson went away and presently returned with a canteen. Charley swallowed the tepid water. "What's going on?" he said.

"The Mexicans have moved back in the church. Some of them are up in the towers shooting at us. A few of them tried to run for the next buildings."

Tried. Charley looked at the blank casual expression on the old man's face. What had the last hour done to him? Edmonson carried his revolver in his fist. Charley got up and handed the canteen back and went to the window nearest him. Norval Douglas looked up and said mildly, "Keep your head back, Charley."

"If I do that I can't see anything."

"What do you want to see? A bullet?"

"All right." He turned back to his corner. Across the room Crabb was in conference with his officers. They seemed to be arguing. A bullet poked a small hole in the back wall; it must have come through one of the windows. Edmonson sat down beside him; his look had turned sour. He said, "How old are you, Charley? Fifteen? Sixteen? You don't belong here."

"Nobody belongs here."

"I suppose not." Douglas fired and the shot was deafening. Edmonson said, "This is ridiculous. We're not savages."

"Aren't we?"

"I hope to God we're not. What's the point of all this? Charley, what in God's name are we doing here?"

His voice had risen. Men were looking at him. Edmonson trailed off and turned his face into the shadows. His plea rang in Charley's ears. Charley felt very calm next to him. He put his hand on the old man's arm. Edmonson looked up, perhaps with gratitude, and got up stiffly to leave. He was muttering when he walked away.

The man at the second window cried out and rolled back from his post. A bullet had seared the top of his shoulder. Charley crawled forward and took that man's place; the injured man went back with two others attending him.

Through the window Charley could see the front of the church. It was a tall two-domed structure. He dragged his rifle up and laid it across the sill, and sat looking out the corner of the opening. He laid his ammunition out beside him on the floor.

A bird flew across the square and some fool shot at it, missing it, and McDowell's voice bawled, "Cut that out!" Charley couldn't see anyone inside the dark windows of the church, but a shot plunked into the wall of the house and he saw a drift of muzzle smoke. Two others fired on it before he cocked his rifle.

"Charley."

It was Bill Randolph, beside him at the next window. Charley said, "What?"

"Nothing," Bill said. When his gun went off it startled Charley. Bill pulled the gun in and began to pour powder down the barrel. He said, "On April eighteenth of 'Forty-seven, I fought under Lieutenant Tom Sweeny at the battle of Cerro Gordo. This ain't the first time I've shot at Mexicans, by God. In August that year I was at Churubusco." Bill carried his battle flags with pride. "I accounted for sixteen greasers at Cerro Gordo," he said. "I didn't count at Churubusco. Ain't none of them can fight worth a damn. I think we ought to bust out of here and pull that Goddamn church down around their ears. Don't know what we're waiting for."

Charley did not know either. Across the room Crabb and the officers were still arguing. The Mexicans fired four or five shots from the church. Charley shot back and reloaded and shot again.

*   *   *

McDowell hunkered on his haunches, glowering at the floor in the center of the little circle of officers. Crabb's indecision so irritated him that he wanted very much to wring the man's neck. On the one hand Crabb was listening to McCoun, who wanted to retreat immediately to the border and give up the whole project. On the other hand he was listening to Holliday, who thought they ought to abandon Caborca and head downstream along the Rio Concepcion to meet Cosby's troops, which by now must be on their way upriver not far away. McDowell's own feeling was that they should storm the church and rout the Mexicans. They had only an inexperienced lieutenant to lead them now that the captain, Rodriguez, was dead on the road

169

between the wheat fields, and the lieutenant obviously had no imagination, since he had done nothing but fort his men up and shoot petulantly across the square. And Crabb was also listening to Colonel Johns, who thought it might be a good idea to wait here for Cosby's army, meanwhile hoping a higher-ranking Mexican officer might arrive and indicate the real intentions of Pesquiera's government. The soldiers in the church were apparently local militia, and had perhaps reacted out of suspicion and unknowing fear. It was not possible to be certain they accurately reflected Pesquiera's own frame of mind.

Crabb sat and talked, and talked. He had an irritating way of going off the subject, and then of returning to it and methodically listing all the advantages and disadvantages of each alternative plan. McDowell had to put down the impulse to shout at him.

For a while Crabb quieted down. McDowell looked bleakly at Lieutenant Will Allen, who answered his look with a dour downturn of his lips. Finally Crabb shook his head, tugged his beard, and said, "Gentlemen, we did not anticipate a reception anything like what happened this morning. I am certain that today's violence was caused by the blundering inexperience of the local officers. I do not believe this hostility represents the feelings of the government. After all, we have a written agreement with Pesquiera, and I have always regarded him as a man of his word. But in spite of that, we are faced with a situation that is patently military in nature. Frankly, I suggest under the circumstances that we allow the military minds to guide our actions. Captain McDowell, what is the West Point answer to our predicament?"

"Attack," McDowell said immediately.

"I tend to agree," Crabb said. McDowell looked at him. Every once in a while the general surprised him. Crabb said, "After all, no matter what the larger picture may be, we have been attacked belligerently and besieged. We are certainly within our rights to retaliate."

"I don't like it," McCoun said flatly. "Men are bound to get hurt, perhaps killed—no, I'll make that stronger: they are bound to get killed." McCoun always talked like the captain of a debating team. No set of circumstances seemed adequate to shake him. He said, "Obviously Mexico is hostile to us. Obviously Pesquiera does not intend to keep his bargain. We have nothing to gain by staying here, except perhaps the satisfaction of stubborn pride. It's folly to do anything but retreat; it's more than folly to attack—it is criminal negligence."

"You are free to voice your opinion," Crabb said coolly. "I for one do not intend to let these people get away with the affront they have presented to us."

"Oh, God," McCoun said softly. McDowell glared at him.

"We are considered enemies here," Crabb said. "None of us can doubt that. We must act accordingly." He stood up and walked to the center of the room, by the piled supplies. He said, "I want your attention."

Men turned to face him, all but those who guarded the windows. Crabb said, "The natives here have seen fit to treat us with malice and violence. They must be taught that this is not acceptable conduct. I propose to lead an attack against the troops in the church. We will charge the convent and gain entrance through that side of the building. I now call for volunteers."

Men looked at one another. McDowell shouldered his rifle and stepped forward, looking around the room with measured contempt. Norval Douglas came away from his post and stood beside him. Jim Woods came up. William Chaney, Clark Small. Bill Randolph came over. Lieutenant Will Allen walked across the room to stand by McDowell. McDowell looked at them one by one. Randolph—that one would go anywhere to find violence. Allen, a good soldier. Chaney—a Nevadan with cool gray eyes and a crippled shoulder. Woods—an ex-saloonkeeper with leather skin and a sure grip on his gun. Clark Small, a nondescript man with a nondescript expression. Norval Douglas—tough and proud. Others came over, some of them reluctantly. He had a glimpse of the boy, Charley Evans, posted by a window with his rifle, looking at Norval Douglas in a strange, uncertain way; but the boy did not move.

"Is this all?" Crabb said.

"I count fifteen of us," McDowell said. "It should be enough."

"All right. Come on," Crabb said.

McDowell pointed to Bill Randolph. "You—bring one of those powder kegs and a slow-match fuse." Then he turned and followed Crabb to the door.

Crabb was businesslike. He took out his revolver and inspected its load, then said, "Give me a hand here," and helped lift down the heavy timber that barred the door. It was a massive wooden door; musket balls would not penetrate it. Crabb looked around. "Is everyone ready?"

"All set," McDowell said. Just before he flung the door open, he had a swift contemptuous look around the room at the fifty-odd men who had not volunteered. They sat packed along the side walls, crouched behind the supply piles, crowded into doorways. He said to the men at the windows, "Lay down a heavy fire against the church to keep their heads down until we're across the plaza." Men came forward out of the shadows and crowded against the windows, some of them looking half-shame-faced but aiming steadily enough through the openings. McDowell said, "Keep your eyes open," and pulled the door open.

A flurry of shots issued from the windows of the long, low-roofed house. McDowell plunged through the doorway, broke out into the sunlight and ran with legs pumping toward the convent. He saw no one in the church windows; the heavy fire had driven the Mexicans back. It was a long run. He slammed up against the convent wall, his back to it and his chest heaving. Crabb and Allen and Randolph were close on his heels; the others were strung out across the square. He whirled and made a low dive through an open window. A woman screamed; there was a succession of gunshots loud in his ears. He saw a Mexican soldier looming with a big-bore musket, and shot the man down point-blank. Someone came in through the window behind him and knocked him down. Women and loud little children were squeezing in panic through a back door. A nun in black stood calmly by the wall, her arms folded. Bill Randolph was standing with his feet spread, leaning forward, pumping shots out of his revolver. McDowell scrambled to his feet, drawing his pistol. A soldier swung through the church door to investigate, wheeled back and pushed the door shut. McDowell ran to it but the door was barred. He heard crashing noises beyond the door— the Mexicans were barricading it with furniture. A little girl ran past him, crying. The nun stooped and picked up the child and carried her outside through the back door. Crabb and Will Allen had crossed the room to guard that door. Bill Randolph was trying to hold onto the powder keg and reload his pistol at the same time. A group of soldiers plunged in through the back door, forcing Crabb and Allen back, firing savagely. McDowell emptied his gun into them and felt his body lurch and buck. The Mexicans retreated and Jim Woods sprang forward to shut the door, but just as he reached it a bullet caught him in the throat and he pitched outward through the doorway. One of the men dragged him back and slammed the door and barred it. When McDowell looked down he saw that his right arm was bleeding profusely; later when he counted the wounds he found that he had been hit nine times in that arm. Most of the wounds were superficial; one bullet had sliced through a muscle and he could not move the arm. He shifted the revolver to his left hand and grimly tried to reload.

Smoke settled down in the convent. Small and Chaney and two others were making a rapid investigation of the rooms. They flushed two children and four nuns and drove them out of the place. Crabb was talking: "Randolph—set that powder keg by the door to the church."

Crabb came across to that door and used a knife to poke a hole in the keg. He inserted the slow-match and tried to ignite it, but by some curious twist of fate it was wet with blood and would not light. Crabb sat down and wrote a note on a leaf of his notebook. Clark Small and Norval Douglas came out of a corridor with a small boy they had caught hiding somewhere. Crabb waved them over to him and said to Douglas, "Tell the boy to take this note across the square. I'm asking them to send back another slow-match fuse for the powder."

"He may not go," Douglas said.

Crabb spoke in the same businesslike tone: "Tell him he'll be shot if he doesn't obey. Tell him to bring back the fuse as quickly as he can."

Douglas relayed the instructions to the boy in Spanish. The boy looked around helplessly with the wild glance of a trapped animal; he took the note and waited by the front door until Douglas opened it for him, and then bolted across the square. Watching all this, McDowell had sunk down with his back against a wall. Waves of weakness came upon him. He looked across the room at Jim Woods, but Woods was dead. Norval Douglas crouched down beside McDowell and ripped off his shirt and made a bandage for the wounded arm. McDowell said weakly, "Thanks."

There was a rending sound in the back of the room. The Mexicans were breaking down the door. Crabb and Douglas wheeled to face that attack and then the splintering door crashed downward, falling on top of Jim Woods's body. Troops rushed in, trampling the door. McDowell grimaced, lay still, and pointed his freshly loaded revolver at the charging Mexicans. They spilled into the room like an overflowing stream of water. Will Allen spun back, wounded somewhere, and fell to the floor. When McDowell lost sight of him in the tangle, Allen was crawling toward the front door.

The Mexicans were shouting like Indians. Powdersmoke made a heavy fog in the room. A small wooden cross was smashed by a bullet and tumbled off its hook on the wall, glancing off McDowell's shoulder. He took aim on a shouting open mouth and fired. The mouth disappeared.

William Chaney, the gray-eyed Nevadan, plunged into the fight with knife and fist, having exhausted his ammunition. Norval Douglas was braced against the wall wielding his reversed rifle like a club, batting Mexicans away with great sweeps. Chaney went down under half a dozen men and died with a knife in his chest. The front door came open, admitting a band of light, and McDowell saw the wounded Allen tumble out through the opening. Crabb, his gun empty, sat down deliberately at the church door and proceeded to reload. McDowell saw a man taking aim on Crabb, and he brought his gun around, but not before the Mexican fired. Crabb took the bullet in his right elbow. McDowell shot the Mexican. Clark Small wheeled and screamed and fell over, his head almost severed from his body by a sword thrust. McDowell glimpsed big Bill Randolph, shouting with huge oaths, wading through the crowd and batting heads together. A dead Mexican fell across McDowell's legs. He grunted and crawled away toward the front door. Crabb was coming that way, backing up slowly, firing at the Mexicans. Individuals were lost in the slurred outlines of the fight. Noise and stench and carnage filled McDowell's senses. Bill Randolph and Norval Douglas stood back to back fighting off attackers. A gun went off and Randolph sagged at the waist; McDowell knew he was dead by the way he fell.

A young Mexican soldier loomed before McDowell. Fear was a glaze on the youth's eyes; his mouth hung open, dragging in air, and a gun hung empty in his hand. McDowell killed the youth with his last shot, and backed out through the doorway. Crabb and Douglas were with him. They picked up Will Allen. Other Americans, pitifully few in number, spun onto the square, coming out through windows and the door. McDowell turned and walked on wavering legs toward the house. The men in the windows there kept up a savage fire, pinning the Mexicans down, preventing pursuit. Crabb and McDowell, with one good arm each, carried Will Allen between them. Guns roared. McDowell looked dismally at Crabb, who had surprised him by his cool display of courage under fire. When they re-entered the big house, someone barred the door behind them. McDowell released Allen to abler hands, and sank slowly to the floor in great weariness. His arm throbbed and he felt an overpowering hunger.

CHAPTER 21

The last thing Charley recalled about Jim Woods was the good-humored remark Woods had made about it being April Fool's Day. He looked out through the window; in the night he could see the outline of the church. The Mexicans had stopped shooting, either because their ammunition was running low, or because they knew that in the dark their muzzle-flashes gave away their locations to American riflemen who were quick to shoot back. And so a cool and threatening truce had settled down. It was past midnight, and Charley's eyes ached. His shift would last another hour before someone would relieve him.

He remembered standing in front of Jim Woods's saloon on a cool rainy morning, just before he had met Norval Douglas. He found himself wanting to know, with a savage desire, what trick of fate it was that had brought such men to this place far from home and killed them without purpose. None of it was fair. He remembered that rainy morning's conversation with Woods; it had been months ago; the words and the voice tones came back to him.

All packed. . . . Going somewhere, Charley?

Back East.

You're doing the Triple Ace out of a chore boy, then.

They'll find another one.

I reckon. . . . Funny-looking moon, all by itself. Tired of the job, Charley?

You might say.

Got money for the trip?

I'll work my passage.

That's a hard row. . . . Good luck to you, then, Charley.

Well, then, he thought, why hadn't he gone back East? What had changed him? Was the future so unimportant that he had just let himself drift into this little unknown war?

Norval Douglas was at his shoulder. Douglas moved without sound, so that he had a way of startling Charley with his sudden appearances. Douglas said quietly, "Trying to get it figured out, kid?"

"Maybe so."

"Maybe you won't, right away. A lot of things don't make sense. It's Jim Woods and Bill, isn't it?"

"How'd you know?"

"It's easy enough to see when a man's thinking. You can learn a lesson from those two."

"What lesson?" Charley asked.

"Bill was a failure. Jim wasn't; he made something out of his life before he died. But he slowed down. The taste went out of life for him. That's why he gave up his business and came along with us. Even if he hadn't been killed, he wouldn't have found anything here that he couldn't have had at home."

"Then what's the point of it?"

"It doesn't make much difference, does it? He had to die somewhere."

Brief anger stirred Charley's lips. "That's all it ever amounts to, isn't it?"

"You don't matter after you're dead," Douglas said. "After you die it's not up to you any more. That's why you've got to make sure you get things done beforehand."

"Aagh," Charley said in disgust. "What if I die tonight?"

"You won't," Douglas told him. "You haven't made your mark yet."

"You've got a lot of faith," Charley said, surprised.

"Well, maybe I do. Faith in myself, faith in you a little."

"And faith that a bullet won't cut me down in the next minute or two."

"There's been enough killing for one day," Douglas said. "Get some rest. I'll watch here for you."

Charley was tired enough not to protest. He went back through the house, past the rooms where the wounded men were abed, and felt his way to a vacant spot on the corridor floor. He lay down with his rifle and canteen at hand. A small flame sputtered nearby and he saw the youth, Carl Chapin, putting a light on the tip of a brown-paper cigarette. Chapin's eyes reflected the little flame frostily. His expression was unfathomable. Charley remembered seeing him at one of the windows during the convent fight, firing savagely at the Mexicans, his lips drawn back in a strange, distorted smile. It made Charley recall the fact that Chapin had once refused to shoot at a jackrabbit.

The red button of the cigarette tip alternately glowed and dimmed in the corridor. Presently it went out in a crush of sparks. Charley put his head back. The floor was hard, he thought; he came awake and it was daylight.

The entire day passed with little more than a peevish exchange of shots. When Charley took his turn at a front window, Crabb and some of the others were in conference; they seemed to have been there all day. McDowell's arm was bandaged from wrist to shoulder, but he was on his feet. Crabb had his own right arm in a sling. Guards were posted at close intervals all the way around the house. Dr. Oxley puttered around the wounded men. Charley spent part of the afternoon dozing in the courtyard, which struck him as an incongruous dark garden; a group of men played cards in the shade of a tree.

During the night a small party slipped out past the corrals to get water from the well. There was a volley of shots, but the men returned with water buckets full, unharmed. A man named Seaton was killed by a random gunshot from the church. Charley stood guard in the early morning hours. His thoughts kept drifting and for an hour he fought out with himself whether he should have volunteered to join the attack on the convent. Nothing made sense.

On the third day a small detachment of Mexican regulars rode in from the south, bringing two small cannon which they set up behind the church. The cannon were not powerful; the general effect of them was noise and a few dents in the front of the house. One ball came through a window, spent, and rolled across the floor; Captain McDowell picked it up in his good hand and tossed it to Norval Douglas. "Feel how hot the damned thing is."

There seemed to be no place closer to the house where the Mexicans were willing to set up their artillery; they probably could not have done so without exposing the cannoneers to American rifle fire. At any rate the cannon stayed where they were and after a short while the Mexicans stopped using up ammunition in them. Nonetheless the rumor trickled around, reaching Charley in midafternoon, that Crabb was worried by the arrival of the regulars, because he had hoped they would lift the siege under Pesquiera's order. Charley learned that evening that some of the officers—Johns and McCoun in particular—wanted to retreat to the border. Crabb, McDowell, Oxley, and a few others were fighting this idea. Charley formed no opinion of his own; he stayed largely by himself.

By the end of the fourth day, the fourth of April, tempers were plainly raw. The men were hungry and word circulated that some of them were willing to overthrow Crabb and let McDowell take over the company and lead a massed attack on the church. To forestall that kind of hasty action, Crabb promised a decision by the following morning. That evening a man called John George was picked off by a Mexican rifleman who had climbed to the roof of a building down the square. George died within a half hour; a small party under Norval Douglas drove the sniper back. After supper the news reached Charley that Lieutenant Will Allen had died in bed of wounds suffered at the battle in the convent. Later on at night, helping to dig graves in the courtyard, he wondered at his own indifference to the deaths around him.

On the morning of April 5, a man whose name Charley did not know deserted. Charley spotted him crawling out between the corral bars with a white piece of cloth affixed to a stick. The man walked nervously across to the church, looking behind him at every few steps. "The son of a bitch," someone said. The deserter was taken into the church. Ten minutes later a single shot boomed within that structure.

Crabb's promised decision was a thick measure of suspense

hanging in the air when at nine o'clock a large body of horsemen entered town from the southwest. A large cry went up among the Mexicans and beyond the church, two blocks down a street, a crowd of women boiled out of shelter to welcome the newcomers. Charley heard the shouts: "*Viva México! Viva Gabilondo!*" The soldiers dismounted and several men ran from the back of the church through the alleys of town to meet the arrivals. Crabb's face had turned worried, then showed a visble relief. Charley kept his post. Men around him were talking excitedly; the prospect of rescue was in the air; but nothing seemed to happen until, almost at noon, a ragged volley of shots issued from the church. At the time, Charley was watching the discussion among the officers, and on the heels of the shots he saw Crabb's face fall. A man in the belfry of the church was hoisting a Mexican flag, and someone shot him down. A stillness settled over the house and Crabb's voice, quiet and calm, was distinctly audible: "I'm afraid that's it."

* * *

Every time he rode horseback, Giron was reminded by the loose bouncing of his paunch of the many bottles of beer he had consumed; a thing which he regretted but did not resolve to change. He stood on the porch of the house they had commandeered, rubbing his hand against his belly, and thought, *Lorenzo Rodriguez is dead. Well, he was not a very good soldier.*

A young lieutenant came quartering across the street and saluted him, reporting: "We have the Americans surrounded, sir."

"Excellent," Giron murmured. "Hold your positions, Lieutenant." He returned the man's salute and went into the house.

Gabilondo had Corella on the carpet. Corella was the stocky ex-miner who had been Lorenzo Rodriguez' lieutenant. He and Gabilondo were of a build and of a size; but Corella's chin was round, not square, and his eyes did not have the flash or intolerance of Gabilondo's.

Gabilondo sat hip-cocked on the edge of a handsomely carved dining table, softly pounding a silver candlestick into his open palm. Lieutenant Corella stood before him at a stiff position of attention; though he was motionless, he seemed to be cringing. Gabilondo was talking, his voice a rasp, when Giron came in.

"Lieutenant, I regard you as a fool and a coward. For five days you have maintained contact with the gringos. You have had them outnumbered by a margin of seven or eight to one. You have had the advantage of two light cannon and superior fire-power and manpower, and superior mobility. And yet what have you done? Nothing. You have retreated into the comforting shelter of the mission-church and plinked occasionally at the gringos. Lieutenant, listen to me!"

"Yes, sir."

"Did you ever once mount an attack against the gringos?"

"No, sir."

"Why not?"

"I had no orders, General."

"In the name of God! Does everything have to be spelled out? Did they not invade our country, shoot down your commanding officer in cold blood, and kill a score of your troops?"

"They did."

"Then why did you not fight back, Lieutenant?"

Corella's chin trembled. "The men—"

"Yes? Yes? Go on, Lieutenant. The men."

"The men were afraid, General."

"Of what? Of a little crowd of gringos whom they outnumbered vastly?"

"Of the Americano rifles. They are much more accurate than our muskets. And the riflemen are expert, General. We have lost half a dozen men to their sniping. The men fear their marksmanship."

"Fool!" Gabilondo shouted. "Coward! You shall pay for this, all of you. I promise it. Now get out of here—out of my sight."

Corella saluted and went. Gabilondo cursed and slammed the silver candlestick into his hand. "Old women," he said. "It is all the fault of Lorenzo Rodriguez. If he had trained his men properly in the first place it might have stiffened their backbones a little. God, I'm sick of cowards and weary of fools. Giron, we must put an end to this matter of the filibusters."

"Sí," said Giron. "I had it in mind that we might offer surrender terms to them."

The candlestick paused in mid-strike and Gabilondo's eyes lifted. He said, after a moment or two, "Just what terms did you have in mind to offer, José?"

"That is not up to me," Giron said immediately.

"There will be no terms," Gabilondo said flatly. "We will attack the house, burn it down, and kill them. That is all. No terms."

"What?" Giron said, taken aback.

Gabilondo showed a thin smile. "My friend José, you are an excellent soldier. I feel we are most fortunate to have you in our army. But in matters of statesmanship you are abysmally ignorant, amigo."

"What does that have to do with it? It is only common humanity to offer them the chance to surrender. It is the only honorable thing—"

"Honor is secondary," Gabilondo interrupted. "We must think first of our country."

"What about our country?"

Gabilondo set the candlestick down. In its place he took out his pistol and began to slap it against his palm. "Whatever the present circumstances may be, we owe our first loyalty to Mexico. Is that not right?"

"Of course. But—"

"Loyalty to Mexico," Gabilondo went on, "is roughly the same as loyalty to our governor, is it not? If we do not honor our leader, we open the door once again to chaos, to revolution, to war and death. You agree?"

"I suppose so. But what has this to do with—"

"José."

"Sí?"

"You will have the kindness to let me finish."

"Sí."

"Let me present to you a picture of what will happen if we allow the filibusters to surrender. First, they will submit to arrest. Second, we will imprison them. Third, they will be brought to trial and prosecuted as enemies of the state, as invaders. True?"

"I suppose so. What's wrong with that?"

"Do you know what will happen if these men are permitted to stand in open court?"

"They will attempt to defend themselves," Giron said. "Unsuccessfully, of course. Then they will be jailed or executed as filibusters. But at least they will have been given a trial. What will we look like if we do not give them that opportunity?"

"Perhaps we will not look good. But I put this to you, José: what will we look like if we do bring them to trial?"

"Honorable men," Giron answered.

"No. For I will tell you what will happen. Brought into court, Señor Crabb will immediately produce the documents which seal his agreements with Pesquiera. The world will then see that Pesquiera has failed to live up to his bargain, has turned against his friends who aided him during his revolution, has shown himself to be an ingrate and a traitor who betrays his allies, and has unlawfully arrested and killed a number of citizens of a foreign power. After that it will not be long before the United States will protest, or perhaps even send troops. The people of Sonora will lose confidence in Pesquiera. They will turn against him. Pesquiera and you and I and all the others will be turned out and spat upon."

Gabilondo laid the pistol down beside his hip and took out a cigar from the humidor on the table. He offered it to Giron; Giron shook his head absently. Gabilondo bit off the end of the cigar and lighted it, and squinted against the smoke. He said quietly, "And so you see, amigo, that we can not permit the filibusters to tell their story in court. They must be silenced."

It was very deep, very involved, very confusing. Giron was a soldier; he was a simple man. He did not like to be drawn into political decisions. He did not understand the implications of political acts. He did not like being put in a position where, no matter what he did, the results might be disastrous for someone. He felt trapped; but his honor forced him to say, "I do not agree. I can not agree. It is honorable to kill on a battlefield.

183

But to murder men who are in a helpless position—that is a mortal sin, General. I can not agree to it."

Gabilondo studied him through half-shuttered eyes. He said softly, "You know, Giron, you are a very valuable man. Not only are you a fine soldier, but you are a man of simple tastes and simple virtues. You are truly a man of the people, amigo. You are a mirror—you reflect the wishes of the people. In your eyes I see all the feelings of the little dirty men and women who work the land. You have taught me something, José, and I am grateful to you for it. It is never wise to go against the wishes of the people. One must always be aware of presenting events in a good light, or the people will rebel." He stood up, away from the table; he picked up his pistol and bounced it in his hand, and holstered it. "Very well," he said, smiling gently. "We shall give them their trial, amigo."

CHAPTER 22

Charley sat with his back to the wall, cradling the rifle between his knees. Crabb was standing by the diminished pile of supplies. The last dim rays of twilight swept across the plaza in swaying shadow. From the church the Mexicans fired occasionally, just often enough to keep the Americans irritated. Crabb talked in a low, level voice, displaying no emotion, none of the histrionic gusto that had marked his earlier speeches. He said:

"The matter is simple enough. This house is completely surrounded. We are outnumbered roughly by a factor of twenty to one. Hilario Gabilondo is here and has made it plain that Pesquiera has turned completely against us. Militarily, our position is hopeless. Gabilondo's truce-bearers have offered us terms of surrender. They are as follows:

"On surrendering, we will be taken to Altar, which is several miles up the river and a larger town than this. There we will be tried as prisoners of war. Gabilondo has several good physicians and has assured us that our wounded will be well attended to. No promises have been made but the implication is that, in view of the touchy nature of our agreements with Pesquiera, the trial will be held quietly and thereafter we will all be escorted under arms to the border, and released on American soil. The details of the surrender are that we will be required to leave the house one by one, leaving our arms behind, and go over to the Mexicans."

He paused, seeming to gather his breath. His head was down, beard against chest; his fingers absently toyed with a button on his vest. He went on: "I might say that Pesquiera's treachery has been a terrible disappointment to me, and I daresay to all of us. I know that many of you had staked your hopes on the promised lands and mineral claims that were to be ours here in Mexico. Instead, men have died here. I offer all of you my profound apologies; I wish I could do more."

He looked up and slowly his gaze traveled around the room. "We have been given till midnight to make up our minds whether we are to surrender. I ask you to think about it and make your answer known to me before that hour."

He nodded sadly and turned, and went out of the room. A dozen heated conversations sprang up immediately; knots of men formed and busy-talking men darted from one group to another. Charley sat still, looking obliquely through the window across the deserted square, turning pale in the wash of moonlight. A bittersweet, faraway expression came into his eyes. A man across the room stood alone praying over a tiny cross in his hands. Norval Douglas stood by a window, rifle in hand, his yellow eyes flickering even in the dimness of night. A shadow nearby was young Carl Chapin, sallow and hollow-eyed, a bandage around the calf of his leg. His lips worked nervously. John Edmonson, old and dried, stood coughing over his bent chest, a pistol hanging forgotten in his hand. The last five days had turned him into a fighter. Charley wondered what good it had done the man. Captain Bob Holliday was relaxing loose-jointed against the wall near Norval Douglas; Holliday looked unconcerned. McDowell was in the center of an angrily arguing group of men. He was holding his injured arm as if it pained him terribly. Charley looked down. He had scars on both hands, from a ricocheting bullet that had sprayed splinters into them. He rubbed his palms against his shirt.

What appeared to be a giant shooting-star flared redly across the square, going overhead in a rush of flame. At his post, Norval Douglas wheeled. "Fire arrow," he shouted. There was a crackle from the roof and when he looked up, Charley saw flames expanding on the thatch roof. Smoke curled downward. Crabb came striding into the room. Fifty men stood and sat, all staring at the growing flame above their heads; Charley felt paralyzed. A chunk of burning thatch fell inward, glancing off a man's shoulder. The man leaped back. Several men rushed forward and began to stamp out the flames. Crabb was shouting for their attention. "Everybody get out of this room! Someone fuse the powder kegs—we'll have to blow the roof off."

Norval Douglas put down his rifle and walked forward deliberately to the corner where the powder kegs were stacked. Charley found himself getting up and following Douglas. Men were streaming out of the room into the back corridors, dragging with them everything they could carry—canteens, guns, food, blankets. By the time Charley carried two kegs to the center of the floor, the room was bright and smoky, and deserted. Douglas looked around and swore softly. "The slow-match fuses are gone."

Charley rushed around in frantic search until he heard Douglas's voice, calm through the thickening smoke: "Never mind, Charley. Bring me a candle."

He took a candle from the big table that they had shoved back against the wall and, not knowing what it was for, carried it to Douglas. He began to choke and cough on the smoke. Douglas dropped the candle to the floor and stamped on it, crushing it, breaking the wax away from the wick. Then he stripped the wick with his fingers and stuck it into the bottom keg. "Get out of here, Charley."

Smoke clogged his lungs; he could not breathe. He turned and staggered blindly. At the edge of the room the smoke was less intense. He found a doorway and went through into a crowd of men. Looking back, he saw Douglas's shape dim in the wavering smoke, weirdly illuminated from above by the clattering flames. A section of thatch fell burning to the floor beyond the powder kegs. Douglas lit the candlewick and wheeled, running forward; but the wick burned quickly and Douglas was not yet to the door when the explosion went off.

The force of it blasted Douglas through the doorway. Charley's head rocked back, recoiling from the terrible noise. Men tumbled around him and he heard brittle objects falling; the room darkened. Douglas, blown flat on the corridor floor, struggled to his knees. His back appeared to have been burned but otherwise he did not seem hurt. A cool draft swept Charley's face and inside the big room he could see that the powder had blown away most of the roof. Two corners still burned, but the flames were small and not powerful enough to do any damage to the adobe walls. Log rafters made naked bars across the night.

*   *   *

"These people," McDowell said firmly, "are determined to destroy us. By surrendering, we'd fall into their hands. Do you honestly think they'll let us go? They can't afford to. If I've got to die in this God-forsaken place, then by Jesus I'm going to sell my life dearly."

"Gabilondo assures me," Crabb murmured in reply, "that he has four sixteen-pound horse-drawn cannon on the way. We can't hold out against him."

"Goddamn it," said McDowell, "I'll take command myself. We can still fight our way out of here."

"Can we?" Crabb retorted. "Gabilondo has half a thousand men—seasoned troops, not green militia any more."

Charley listened to all this with detached bitterness. He looked up past the scorched rafters at the star-patterned sky. Smoke still hung in his nostrils. Crabb said firmly, "We can't divide the party. It would do neither of us any good, McDowell, if half of us surrendered and the other half attempted to make a fight of it. Only if the whole party surrenders at once will they treat us as prisoners of war. It's better I assure you not to rankle them by useless resistance. I'm satisfied with the terms; I advise we surrender."

"I'll second," McCoun said in a wooden tone.

McDowell threw up his hand and grimaced, and turned away. Norval Douglas joined him and the two tall men conversed in quiet tones. Crabb pulled out a pocket watch from his vest and squinted at it, and shook his head, handing the watch to Mc-Coun, who read the time and handed it back. Crabb snapped it shut, pocketed it, and said, "Men, it's now eleven o'clock. I intend to surrender the party."

A murmur ran around the room but no one spoke in protest. There was, in fact, a tangible measure of relief in the air. Mc-Dowell and Douglas moved back to the far wall, both of them carrying their guns, and stood resolutely there. Charley could see what was on their minds. He went across to them. McDowell gave him a curious look, but it was Douglas who put his hand on Charley's shoulder and shook his head. Charley said defiantly, "It's not my fault if they're all cowards."

"They're not cowards," Douglas said. "They just don't believe that what's here is worth fighting for. You can't blame them."

"Then why are you staying?"

"We'll try and make a break for the river after you've all left. If we can steal a pair of horses, we'll be all right."

"Why take the chance?" Charley said. "In a day or two we'll all be loose."

"Probably. But I didn't sign on just to surrender. It's hard to explain, Charley. Just take my word for it."

"I guess I'll stay," Charley said, feeling the dampness of his palms.

"No. Get out of here with the rest of them."

"Listen," Charley said, "don't commit suicide. Come on out with the rest of us."

Douglas shook his head gently. "You've got a chance, Charley, to make something out of your life, because you're young. The rest of them don't."

"What about you?"

"If you live for something, you've got to have the decency to die for it. Get out of here, Charley." Douglas spoke the last five words with hard energy, as if by his viciousness he hoped to persuade. When Charley didn't move, Douglas said, "I don't want you here, Charley. Do you understand that? If you stay, and we don't make it, your death will be on my hands. Don't do that to me."

Charley looked away, disappointed—for at this moment Douglas, who relied on no one, was pleading with him. "Go on," Douglas said softly. Charley turned away and moved like a mechanism toward the men who were lining up by the front door, discarding their weapons. When he looked back, Douglas and McDowell were gathering up abandoned revolvers, jamming them into their belts.

Crabb was at the head of the line. His arm in a white sling was a pale triangle. He said, "All right. Open the door." Someone lifted the bar down. Crabb pulled the door open. For a stretching interval, no one spoke, no one moved; and nothing stirred on the plaza. Crabb took up a white flag and stepped out.

Through a window Charley saw him cross the square, saw two Mexican soldiers come out to meet him, saw them take him away.

The night was deep and still. Singly, men walked through the door and across the dusty square. It was a long walk. Charley, last in line, looked back and in the shadows saw two lean figures standing. He looked down, scuffed his feet, and went out.

The Mexicans searched them and tied them up in a long storehouse beyond the church. Crabb was not tied; he stood off in a corner between two guards. Old John Edmonson sat down wearily beside Charley and scratched his face with his bound-together hands. He said, "Unfortunate, very unfortunate."

Charley covered his face with his hands and thought darkly of two tall figures in the gloom. Over the mutter of conversations he heard a sudden flurry of gunshots, a ragged after volley, and a thick silence. In the distance someone shouted, "*Viva México!*" And outside the storehouse, a voice spoke heartily: "*Tendrimas cadaveres Yanquis, con que engordar a nuestros puercos.*" And back in the black shadows one of the prisoners said hoarsely, "Our hogs will fatten on the carcasses of the Yankees."

"Jesus Christ."

"What do you suppose they'll do to us?"

"The sons of bitches. Maybe we shouldn't have trusted them."

"Crabb, you bastard, it's all your fault. None of this would have happened if it hadn't been for you."

"By God, Crabb, if I get loose from here I'll hunt you down and so help me I'll stick a knife in you."

"I suppose your own greed had nothin' to do with it, hey, Shorty?"

"Go to hell, Hyne."

"Gentlemen," Crabb said softly, "if we emerge safely from this, I shall put myself at your disposal."

"Goddamn right you will," said Shorty's voice in the gloom.

"Oh, Mother of God!"

"Did you hear those shots? They must have killed McDowell and Douglas. Goddamned fools, those two."

"I wish that Zimmerman son of a bitch was here. This would make him a nice fat story for the *Times*, all right."

Anonymous voices in the black. Charley tried not to listen to them. In a little while a Mexican officer came in and took Crabb away with him. A silence enveloped the building; he could hear the uneven breathing of men around him. Somebody said quietly, "Hey—*soldado*. You got a drink? *Agua?*" The guards made no answer.

*   *   *

Giron sat in the stuffing of a faded red sofa and watched the pistol slap steadily against Gabilondo's palm. Gabilondo went around the desk and sat down behind it. Crabb stood stiffly in the center of the room, an armed soldier behind each shoulder. His right arm hung in a bandage-sling. He looked like a mild, everyday sort of man, Giron thought, not like a raging filibuster at all. In a moment a line of junior officers filed into the room and ranked themselves along the wall. "This," Gabilondo murmured to Crabb with a gesture, "is your jury, amigo. You are here to be tried by a court-martial."

"I thought we were to be tried at Altar."

"I have changed my mind," Gabilondo said. Giron followed his English with difficulty; he was surprised that Gabilondo showed the courtesy to speak in Crabb's tongue.

"Am I not entitled to counsel?" Crabb asked. Giron admired his haughty, unbending demeanor.

"As a man of varied political background," Gabilondo said, "you are no doubt perfectly capable of speaking in your own behalf, señor."

"Very well," Crabb said. The junior officers stood blankly at attention. Giron stood up, not wishing to draw attention to himself, and moved around beside the sofa where he could put his shoulder blades to the wall. He folded his hands before him.

"You are charged," Gabilondo said, "with illegal invasion, with acts tantamount to an act of war, and with willful murder. How do you plead?"

"Not guilty."

"To each charge?"

"Yes. To each charge."

"The evidence is as follows," Gabilondo said. His voice rang hollowly under the high ceiling. "At the head of a band of armed men, you entered the state of Sonora from a foreign territory, intending to invade by force of arms. When halted by a regularly appointed officer of the government army, you informed him that you intended to advance in spite of the fact that he ordered you to withdraw. Then you shot the same officer, without warning, and inflicted a state of siege upon the members of the local militia. Now, these are all facts, señor. I do not see how you can plead innocence when the facts are so plain."

"The facts as you state them are incomplete."

"Ah," Gabilondo said, and smiled. "How so, señor?"

"We are here not as illegal invaders, but as friendly colonists who were invited to settle here by your state government."

"I see," Gabilondo said. "You no doubt have proof of this allegation?"

"I do." Crabb reached awkwardly into his vest with his left hand and pulled out an oilskin pouch. From this he extracted a sheaf of papers and stepped forward to place them on Gabilondo's desk. Gabilondo picked up the papers and made a show of reading them. It took some time. Giron was aware of the rise and fall of his own chest, the flicker of oil in the lamps, the sleepy attention of the junior officers who were probably longing to return to their blankets and go to sleep. A young lieutenant sat back at a small writing table under a lamp, taking down testimony. His expression was bored, tired; he had marched for a week. Giron was thirsty for beer. He licked his lips.

"Forgeries," Gabilondo said in a bland tone. "Naturally you would prepare yourself with such so-called documentary evidence before embarking on such a ruthlessly daring expedition. But this signature is definitely not that of Ignacio Pesquiera, and for myself, señor, I deny ever having affixed my signature to such a paper."

Crabb stood calmly and said nothing.

Gabilondo took the hood off the desk lamp. Crabb said, "The documents are not forgeries, General, and you know that fact as well as I. We were both present when they were signed."

"Your memory must be at fault, señor," Gabilondo murmured, and set a corner of the sheaf of papers afire. He let them burn up until the flames reached his fingers; then he dropped them on the desk and let the flames consume the last corners. "So much for that evidence," he said. "Have you anything else to say in your defense?"

"Only that I am innocent, that you know I am innocent, and that if the people of Sonora ever discover what treacherous dogs they have elected in you and Pesquiera, you will both find yourselves rotting in the earth." Crabb's words were forceful; his voice was calm. He seemed to recognize the futility of protest. Giron looked away and studied the crucifix on the wall.

Gabilondo turned to the lieutenant at the writing table. "You may strike the defendant's last remark from the record, Lieutenant."

"Sí, General."

Crabb said, "You may do with me as you wish, General. I do not deny that my motives may have been base. But I ask that you honor your terms of surrender to my men. They did not come here expecting to fight against troops. They had no political objectives in mind. They are innocent of any crime against the state. I hold you to your word to release them on American soil."

"Your heroics are touching, amigo," Gabilondo murmured. "But I have the feeling that the spirit of filibustering remains strong in the barbaric hearts of your countrymen north of the border. I believe they need a lesson. It is time they learned that Mexico is not a savage free land open to the greedy clutchings of misguided filibusters. We are a sovereign people, señor, and it is time the United States was made aware of that fact."

"Marvelous sentiments," Crabb drawled. Giron cringed; he wished the man would break down.

"Gentlemen of the jury," Gabilondo said, his tone as dry as the desert winds, "I will have your verdict."

One of the junior officers nodded his head. Gabilondo said, "It is the verdict of a jury of regularly appointed officers that you are guilty of the charges brought against you by the state. Have you anything to say before I prescribe punishment?"

"Nothing," Crabb said.

"Then it is the sentence of this court-martial that you and your followers be executed by rifle fire at dawn."

Giron felt he should speak. He looked at the slitted eyes of Gabilondo and held his tongue. He was very thirsty and wondered if the cantina was still open to the soldiers. He would go there afterward and drink enough beer to knock him out.

"*Adios*, Señor Crabb," Gabilondo murmured.

"I doubt," Crabb said, "that you can know the consequences of this inhuman act, General." He turned on his heel and went out between the two silent guards.

"Very well, José," said Gabilondo. "Are you satisfied? The trial has been held. The verdict goes on record."

Giron said nothing. He picked up his hat and sword and turned to the door, flicking his dry tongue around his teeth. It was better not to mix in political things.

CHAPTER 23

Crabb was returned to the barracks at one o'clock in the morning; he was kept by himself and was not allowed to communicate with the men. Charley lay awake and listened to the snoring of a man nearby. Someone came in with a lamp and a Mexican read in halting English the official sentence of the court-martial, that the entire company was to be shot at sunrise. A dozen guards stood at the front with shotguns. Several more lamps were brought. Charley saw bearded faces, open red mouths, weeping eyes; men cursed and men cried; some just sat. In half an hour some soldiers came in and looked around and picked out the sallow youth, Carl Chapin, and took him outside with them. Soon they returned and Chapin walked directly to Charley. "He's younger than I am," Chapin said, and went back to fade into the crowd. The soldiers took Charley with them and sudden fear made his legs go limp; he concentrated all his attention on a livid hatred of Chapin.

But the soldiers only took him back to the big adobe house with its roof blown off where he had spent the previous days in siege. Nine of the wounded were there, and Charley remained under guard until just before dawn a man came and took him to another large house beyond the church. A squat, powerful man in a creased uniform took him by the arm and sat him down and spoke brusquely. "My name is Hilario Gabilondo. I am in charge here. What is your name?"

"Charles Evans."

"Your date of birth?"

"December twenty-fifth, Eighteen Forty-two."

"Christmas Day, eh?"

"Yes."

"You are the youngest of the party, then."

"I guess I am. What about it?"

"We have decided to spare one from among you," Gabilondo said. "As the youngest, you have been chosen. I trust you will be thankful for your good fortune."

"Yeah," Charley said numbly.

"Eventually," Gabilondo continued, "you will be released to return to your country. You understand it is a gesture of mercy on our part to show that we are not wolves here. I shall expect you to make a full report of what has happened here to the American newspapers—so that your countrymen will know better than to try invading Mexico again."

Charley said nothing. He hoped his expression was as cool as he intended it to be; he had that much caring left. In the past few hours he had not thought much about anything. He knew he was thirsty and hungry and in need of sleep, but those things did not matter. Nothing mattered.

They took him outside and put him on a horse amid a column of soldiers.

*　　*　　*

The window was high; the only thing he could see through it was sky. For hours he would watch clouds drift across, their shapes slowly changing. There were two cots in the cell, nailed to the floor, but Charley was alone. There was a tiny barred opening in the door. All he could see through it was the dim adobe wall on the far side of the jail corridor. With busy fingers he tied knots in pieces of straw that he had taken from the mattress ticking. The floor at his feet was littered with little bits of broken straw.

Once in a while he would tell himself he was lucky to be alive.

Usually he did not believe it. Lucky or unlucky, he did not know, what difference was there?

One afternoon the door opened and someone stumbled into the dim room. The door closed quickly and tumblers clicked. Charley squinted up through the gloom.

"Evans," the man said hoarsely. "Evans?"

"Yes."

"My God. I thought they were all dead." It was, Charley saw, Sus Ainsa.

"No," Charley said, "not all of them." He saw the tracks of pain and anger etched into Sus' face and suddenly he wished very much that he could also be able to feel those things. He felt nothing.

Sus lurched to the opposite cot and lowered himself onto it. He sat with his elbows on his knees, hands dangling, jaw slack. He shook his head, blinked, and said, "How long have you been here?"

"I don't know. I didn't bother to start counting. Sooner or later they'll let me out and send me back across the Line."

"Lucky," Sus said.

"Sure."

"Were—" Sus began, and stopped to clear his throat, and began again: "Were you there?"

"Not when they executed them."

"Oh," Sus said.

"I was there afterward," Charley said, finding himself unable to put tone into his voice. "It was the third day after the execution, I think. They took me back—they said they wanted me to have a good look."

"Who took you?"

"Gabilondo."

Sus looked searchingly at him, as if he wanted Charley to go on, or rather, as if he didn't truly want him to go on but had to know, and so Charley said, "The Mexicans hadn't buried anybody. I guess maybe they were too busy celebrating the victory. The smell was pretty bad and we couldn't get too close. It looked like the bodies had been chewed by animals, and I guess the pigs got at them. I saw a finger on the ground, I suppose they cut it off for a ring. I recognized McCoun and a few of the others. The people in town were wearing our people's clothes. They had General Crabb's head in a jar of vinegar, you know—a Mexican showed it to me. They made me wear a red jacket and dance around in the square."

Sus said nothing. After a stretch of dark silence he said tentatively, "I got word that they wiped out McKinney and his sixteen men. I guess they made a complete job of it. Eighty-odd men, and two of us left alive, Charley." Sus looked as if he wanted to continue, but Charley gave him no encouragement. Sus said only, "They let me write a letter to my sister but I couldn't think of what to tell her."

Neither of them spoke again. Outside, through the window Charley could see the heavy dark hang of thick clouds. At sundown a guard brought supper for them; Charley ate because it gave him something to do. Then he lay back and watched the small square patch of sky darken. There was a brief hole in the clouds through which stars winked like distant lamplit windows across the desert, brightening one by one until the overcast swept by and obliterated them.

Every once in a while, at times like this one, he would think back on the night before the execution and remember young Chapin, pale and bent over his racking cough. Chapin had given Charley life by sacrificing his own: Why? Charley wondered if it meant there was something he should do with his gift of life. But none of them were there to answer him; only Sus was there, and Sus had not known the final truth of that night of surrender. Sus had been spared, probably because he was Mexican himself and had friends among the men of power. Sus had not been given the choice: it was Crabb who had chosen one way, Douglas and McDowell who had chosen the other. Each had chosen freely and the same fate had come to all of them.

Sus' voice cut across his thoughts: "Evans?"

"What?"

"I guess this all sits pretty hard with you."

"And?"

"Don't make up your mind too fast," Sus said to him.

"About what?"

"You've got plenty of time," Sus said. "Don't let what you've seen turn you into a rock. The only thing you have is the future. The past is dead for all of us. It was something like this that made Norval Douglas what he was—but it didn't do him any good to lose his faith."

Faith in what? was the answer that hung on Charley's tongue, but he did not voice it. Sus' talk droned on, insistent:

"Loneliness is the worst thing of all."

Like ghosts they made visions before Charley: Edmonson, Chapin, Bill Randolph, Parker, Woods, Crabb, McKinney, McCoun, Holliday, McDowell, Douglas. Which was important: That each of them had lived, or that they had died? Who was at fault, Crabb for trusting too much, or Douglas and McDowell for refusing to give up? And why was Charley alive tonight? There ought to be a reason for it, beyond the random fact that he had been the youngest. Perhaps when he was released he might go and have a look for that reason. He doubted he would ever find it, but it would be as good a way to pass the time as any.

Across the cell, Sus spoke: "You awake?"

Charley almost answered, but he could think of nothing to say to Sus. He turned his face toward the black wall. It was beginning to rain.

EPILOGUE

After his release from Mexico in September 1857, six months after the execution at Caborca, Charley Evans disappeared into the Southwestern desert. No one is recorded to have seen him for forty years. During that interval a Civil War was fought; the Indian tribes were subdued; railroads and telegraph threaded all quarters of the West; the day of the cattleman came, thrived briefly, and went, superseded by the day of the homestead farmer; the legendary plainsmen and gunfighters lived and died, leaving their myths; automobiles and telephones appeared. In 1897, weathered and gray, Charley Evans walked into Yuma leading a burro. He had been prospecting, but what he had been searching for in the desert for forty years was not clear, and he did not choose to reveal it. When he left Yuma to walk back into the desert it was almost the turn of the century. He was never seen again. The world had forgotten the executions at Caborca.

After Charley left Mexico, Sus Ainsa was brought before a Mexican tribunal in a long, involved mockery of a trial, and was finally released in the absence of a verdict. He spent years trying to clear his name, and subsequently joined his brother, Augustin, in developing a prosperous coal business in Sonora. During those decades Ignacio Pesquiera, although widely disliked, continued to rule the state of Sonora. There was no particular difference between his brand of despotism and Gandara's.

After Crabb's death, according to one source, letters from William Walker were found among his papers, proving that the two filibuster chiefs had entertained the idea of conquering the whole of Mexico: Crabb to work south from the Arizona border, Walker to work north from Central America. On May 1, 1857, or only about three weeks after the Crabb expedition met disaster, William Walker, the last surviving filibuster, surrendered to U. S.

Navy Commander Charles H. Davis, in order to avoid death at the hands of Nicaraguans and Costa Ricans who had risen against Walker's piratical regime. Thus ended Walker's scheme, but not his covetousness: again in 1860 he invaded Honduras with a filibuster force, but was captured and executed on September 12 of that year.

Immediately following the execution of the Crabb expedition, General Gabilondo sent Lieutenant Corella north from Caborca with three hundred troops to engage the party of twenty-six gringos who were coming down from Tucson to reinforce Crabb. This relief column included in its roster some respected Indian fighters and even Granville H. Oury, who was to become a powerful figure in Southwestern politics. Despite its fighting ability, however, the column was outnumbered twelve to one. Corella attacked, and the column was driven back across the border in confusion and hardship. It was a grim retreat; two or three men died.

Crabb's was the last armed filibustering expedition to attempt the conquest of Mexico. In the absence of evidence that might have proved that there had been agreements between Pesquiera and Crabb, the United States government had no recourse but to let the issue drop after formally protesting the incident. (In fact copies of the agreement documents existed, but were only discovered much later.) John Forsyth, the American Envoy and Minister Plenipotentiary to Mexico, lodged a strong protest of the execution with Pesquiera and with the government at Mexico City. In Washington, on February 12, 1858, President James Buchanan transmitted to the House of Representatives the Secretary of State's report on the Crabb expedition: Executive Document 64, 35th Congress, 1st Session.

The issue was dropped; the incident soon became one of the minor, forgotten wars of our history. Today there remain the tall palms of Caborca, a few yellowed documents, and the dusty bronze plaque on the face of the battle-scarred church.